KETO DIET

COOKBOOK

FOR BEGINNERS

135 Easy-to-Make Delicious,
Low-Carb & High-Fat Recipes
To Be Healthy and Looking Great
• Includes Color Photos •

Mia Norman

Disclaimer
The information provided in this cookbook is for general informational purposes only. All recipes and nutritional information are offered in good faith and are believed to be accurate at the time of publication. However, the author makes no representation or warranty of any kind, express or implied, regarding the accuracy, adequacy, validity, reliability, availability, or completeness of any information contained in this cookbook.

The recipes in this cookbook are intended for educational and entertainment purposes. Always consult with a qualified healthcare professional or nutritionist before starting any new diet or exercise program, especially if you have pre-existing medical conditions, are pregnant, nursing, or are taking medication. The author and publisher disclaim any liability for any adverse effects or consequences resulting from using the recipes or suggestions herein.

Individual results may vary. The nutritional information provided is estimated and can vary depending on the ingredients and brands used. Readers are encouraged to seek professional advice regarding specific health or dietary concerns.

By using this cookbook, you accept this disclaimer in full.

Table of Contents:

Introduction……………………………….. 5

CHAPTER 1: Basics of the Diet…………….. 5

The Three Essential Macronutrients

of the Keto Diet…………………………… 5

Health Benefits of the Keto Diet……………… 5

Keto Flu: Symptoms and Remedies…………… 6

Common Myths and Misconceptions…………. 6

CHAPTER 2: Getting Started with Keto……. 7

Techniques, Tips, and Tricks………………… 7

What to Eat and Avoid……………………… 8

Embracing the Keto Lifestyle………………… 9

CHAPTER 3: Keto Breakfasts……………… 11

1. Avocado and Bacon Breakfast Bowl………… 12

2. Keto Spinach and Feta Omelette…………… 12

3. Cauliflower Hash Browns………………… 13

4. Egg and Cheese Breakfast Muffins………… 13

5. Chia Seed Pudding with Berries…………… 14

6. Low-Carb Breakfast Casserole…………… 14

7. Keto Pancakes with Butter and Syrup………. 15

8. Sausage and Egg Breakfast Skillet………… 15

9. Keto French Toast……………………… 16

10. Smoked Salmon and Avocado

Eggs Benedict……………………………. 16

11. Keto Waffles………………………… 17

12. Mushroom and Cheese Omelette………… 17

13. Keto Cinnamon Rolls………………… 18

14. Scrambled Eggs with Cream Cheese……… 18

15. Low-Carb Bagels with Cream Cheese……… 19

16. Zucchini Fritters……………………… 19

17. Keto Breakfast Pizza………………… 20

18. Keto Shakshuka……………………… 20

19. Ham and Cheese Frittata……………… 21

20. Green Eggs and Ham………………… 21

21. Keto Cottage Cheese Pancakes…………… 22

22. Keto Breakfast Rolls………………… 22

CHAPTER 4: Keto Salad & Soup Recipes….. 23

1. Greek Chicken Salad…………………… 24

2. Keto Cobb Salad……………………… 24

3. Avocado and Bacon Salad……………… 25

4. Taco Salad with Avocado Dressing………… 25

5. Creamy Cauliflower Soup……………… 26

6. Chicken Zoodle Soup………………… 26

7. Keto Egg Drop Soup …………………… 27

8. Asian Chicken Salad…………………… 27

9. Creamy Mushroom Soup………………… 28

10. Shrimp and Avocado Salad……………… 28

CHAPTER 5: Poultry Recipes……………… 29

1. Garlic Butter Chicken Thighs……………… 30

2. Keto Chicken Alfredo…………………… 30

3. Buffalo Chicken Wings…………………… 31

4. Keto Chicken Parmesan………………… 31

5. Bacon-Wrapped Chicken Breast…………… 32

6. Keto Chicken Tikka Masala……………… 32

7. Stuffed Chicken Breast

with Spinach and Cheese………………… 33

8. Chicken Zucchini Boats………………… 33

9. Keto BBQ Chicken……………………… 34

10. Herb Roasted Turkey Breast……………… 34

11. Chicken Bacon Ranch Skillet…………… 35

12. Keto Orange Chicken…………………… 35

13. Keto Chicken Teriyaki………………… 36

14. Keto Kung Pao Chicken………………… 36

CHAPTER 6: Pork Recipes……………….. 36

1. Garlic Butter Pork Chops……………… 37

2. Keto Pulled Pork……………………… 38

3. Keto Pork Schnitzel…………………… 38

4. Keto BBQ Ribs……………………… 39

5. Bacon-Wrapped Pork Loin……………… 39

6. Italian Sausage and Peppers……………… 40

7. Pork Stuffed Peppers…………………… 40

8. Keto Pork Meatballs…………………… 41

9. Creamy Mushroom Pork Chops………….. 41

10. Keto Pork Tacos……………………… 42

11. Mustard-Crusted Pork Chops…………… 43

12. Keto Sweet and Sour Pork……………… 43

CHAPTER 7: Beef & Lamb Recipes……….. 45

1. Keto Beef Stroganoff…………………… 46

2. Garlic Herb Crusted Lamb Chops ………… 46

3. Keto Shepherd's Pie…………………… 47

4. Grilled Ribeye Steak…………………… 47

5. Keto Meatloaf………………………… 48

6. Moroccan Spiced Lamb………………… 48

7. Keto Philly Cheesesteak………………… 49

8. Keto Burger with Cheese and Bacon……….. 49

Table of Contents:

9. Lamb Kofta Kebabs………………… 50
10. Keto Beef Bourguignon………………… 50
CHAPTER 8: Fish & Seafood Recipes ……… 51
1. Lemon Garlic Butter Shrimp ……………… 52
2. Coconut Shrimp………………… 52
3. Keto Fish Tacos.………………… 53
4. Garlic Butter Scallops............ ………… 53
5. Keto Crab Cakes.………………… 54
6. Keto Salmon Patties.………………… 54
7. Seared Ahi Tuna.………………… 55
8. Keto Clam Chowder.………………… 55
9. Blackened Salmon.………………… 56
10. Crab Stuffed Mushrooms ……………… 56
CHAPTER 9: Vegan, Vegetables
& Vegetarian Recipes ……………………… **57**
1. Keto Cauliflower Mac and Cheese………… 58
2. Bacon-Wrapped Asparagus ……………… 58
3. Keto Zucchini Fries.………………… 59
4. Keto Mashed Cauliflower.....……………… 59
5. Cheesy Baked Zucchini.………………… 60
6. Cauliflower Rice Pilaf.………………… 60
7. Keto Ratatouille.………………… 61
8. Spinach Artichoke Dip.………………… 61
9. Keto Avocado Pesto Zoodles ……………… 62
10. Spicy Cauliflower Bites.……...………… 62
11. Vegan Keto Curry.………………… 63
12. Cauliflower Pizza Crust.………………… 63
13. Keto Tofu Stir Fry.………………… 64
14. Eggplant Lasagna.………………… 64
CHAPTER 10: Asian Stile Recipes…………... 65
1. Keto Miso Soup ………………… 66
2. Shrimp Pad Thai.………………… 66
3. Zoodle Lo Mein.………………… 67
4. Keto Thai Green Curry.………………… 67
5. Spicy Beef Lettuce Wraps ……………… 68
6. Keto Chicken Satay..... ……………… 68
CHAPTER 11: Sides & Snacks Recipes……….. 69
1. Keto Cheese Crisps.………………… 70
2. Parmesan Zucchini Chips ……………… 70
3. Keto Mozzarella Sticks.………………… 71

4. Avocado Fries.………………… 71
5. Garlic Butter Shrimp Skewers.……………… 72
6. Keto Onion Rings ... ………………… 72
CHAPTER 12: Desserts & Sweet Treats
Recipes ……………………………... **73**
1. Almond Flour Brownies.………………… 74
2. Keto Cheesecake Bites.……...………… 74
3. Coconut Fat Bombs.………………… 75
4. Keto Lemon Bars.………………… 75
5. Raspberry Cream Cheese Bars.……...…… 76
6. Pecan Pie Bars.………………… 76
7. Keto Strawberry Shortcake ……………… 77
8. Keto Chocolate Truffles.……...………… 77
9. Pumpkin Spice Muffins.………………… 78
10. Keto Apple Pie.………………… 78
CHAPTER 13: Bread Recipes……………… 79
1. Almond Flour Bread.………………… 80
2. Cheddar Garlic Biscuits ……………… 80
3. Flaxseed Bread.………………… 81
4. Herb and Cheese Bread.………………… 81
5. Zucchini Bread.……...………… 82
6. Cauliflower Breadsticks.………………… 82
BONUS CHAPTER: Sauces & Dressing
Recipes……………………………………… **83**
Conclusion:
Embrace the Keto Journey………………... **90**

INTRODUCTION

The Keto Diet, short for "ketogenic diet," is a popular eating plan that has gained significant attention for its potential health benefits and unique approach to nutrition. Unlike many diets focusing on calorie counting or portion control, the Keto Diet emphasizes macronutrient balance, exceptionally high fat, moderate protein, and deficient carbohydrate intake. This shift in dietary composition aims to induce a metabolic state known as ketosis, where the body burns fat for fuel instead of carbohydrates. Originating from therapeutic uses in the early 20th century, particularly for epilepsy, the Keto Diet has evolved into a versatile approach for weight management, enhanced mental clarity, and overall health improvements.

CHAPTER 1: Basics of the Diet

The Three Essential Macronutrients of the Keto Diet:

• **Fats:** Approximately 70-80% of daily calories come from fats. These include healthy fats like avocados, nuts, seeds, olive oil, and fatty fish, which are essential for maintaining energy levels and supporting bodily functions.

• **Proteins:** Around 25-30% of calories are derived from proteins, which include meats, poultry, eggs, and dairy products. Adequate protein intake helps maintain muscle mass while ensuring that excess protein does not disrupt the state of ketosis.

• **Carbohydrates:** Carbohydrate intake is restricted to about 5-10% of daily calories, often below 50 grams per day. This limited intake of carbs forces the body to switch from glucose metabolism to fat metabolism, producing ketones that serve as an alternative energy source

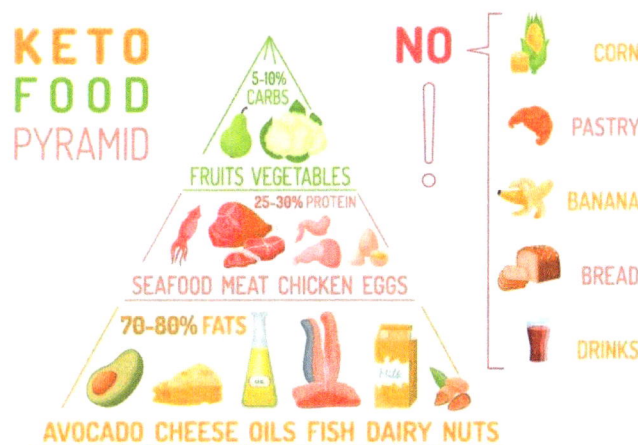

Health Benefits of the Keto Diet

1. Weight Loss and Metabolic Health

One of the most celebrated benefits of the keto diet is its effectiveness in promoting weight loss. By reducing carbohydrate intake, the body burns fat energy stores, leading to weight loss. This process is accompanied by a decrease in insulin levels, which not only aids in fat loss but also helps prevent insulin resistance—a condition linked to obesity and type 2 diabetes.

2. Cardiovascular Health

The keto diet can improve markers of cardiovascular health. Studies have shown that individuals on the keto diet often experience reductions in triglyceride levels, increases in HDL (good) cholesterol, and reductions in LDL (bad) cholesterol. These changes contribute to a lower risk of heart disease and stroke.

3. Blood Sugar and Diabetes Management

The keto diet can be particularly beneficial for individuals with type 2 diabetes. By significantly reducing carbohydrate intake, the diet helps manage blood sugar levels more effectively than traditional low-fat diets. This stabilization of blood sugar can reduce the need for medication and prevent complications associated with diabetes.

4. Enhanced Cognitive Function and Mood

The keto diet is not just beneficial for physical health; it also supports mental and emotional well-being. When fueled by ketones rather than glucose, the brain often experiences improved clarity, focus, and cognitive function. This can be particularly beneficial for individuals dealing with cognitive impairments or conditions like epilepsy and Alzheimer's disease.

5. Mood Stabilization and Emotional Well-being

The keto diet has been associated with improved mood and reduced symptoms of anxiety and depression. The stable blood sugar levels and steady energy supply provided by a keto diet can prevent mood swings and enhance overall emotional stability. Additionally, many people report better sleep quality, further improving mental health.

Keto Flu: Symptoms and Remedies

When transitioning to a keto diet, some people experience flu-like symptoms, known as the keto flu. Symptoms may include headache, fatigue, dizziness, and nausea. To minimize these effects:

Stay Hydrated: Drink plenty of water.
Replenish Electrolytes: Consume foods rich in sodium, potassium, and magnesium.
Gradual Transition: Slowly reduce carb intake rather than drastically changing overnight.

Tracking Your Progress

1. Using Apps and Journals

Tracking your food intake and progress can help you stay on track with your keto diet. Use apps or journals to log your meals, monitor your macronutrient intake, and note any changes in your weight and health.

2. Measuring Ketone Levels

To ensure you're in ketosis, consider measuring your ketone levels using urine strips, blood meters, or breath analyzers. This can provide feedback on how well you adhere to the diet and whether any adjustments are needed.

Common Myths and Misconceptions

There are several myths and misconceptions about the keto diet that can be confusing. Here are a few common ones:

Myth: The keto diet is a high-protein diet.
   Reality: The keto diet is moderate in protein. Consuming too much protein can prevent the body from entering ketosis.
Myth: The keto diet is only for weight loss.
   Reality: While weight loss is a common benefit, the keto diet can also improve overall health and manage Various medical conditions.
Myth: You can eat unlimited amounts of fat on a keto diet.
   Reality: While fat intake is higher on a keto diet, it is essential to maintain a caloric balance and choose Healthy fats.

CHAPTER 2:
Getting Started with Keto

How to Transition to a Keto Diet

Transitioning to a keto diet involves gradually reducing carbohydrate intake while increasing fat consumption. Start by cutting out high-carb foods like bread, pasta, and sugary snacks. Replace them with healthy fats like avocados, nuts, and oils. Ensure adequate hydration and electrolyte intake to ease the transition and avoid the "keto flu."

Techniques, Tips, and Tricks

Transitioning to and maintaining a keto diet can be challenging without the right strategies. Here are some techniques, tips, and tricks to help you succeed on your keto journey:

Techniques:

1. **Meal Planning and Preparation**

   Planning and preparing your meals in advance is essential for staying on track:
   - Weekly Planning: Create a meal plan to ensure keto-friendly options are ready.
   - Batch Cooking: Prepare large meals and snacks to save time during busy days.
   - Portion Control: Use a food scale to accurately measure portions and track macronutrient intake.

2. **Cooking Methods**

   Utilize cooking methods that enhance the flavor and nutritional value of keto foods:
   - Grilling: Perfect for meats and vegetables.
   - Roasting: Brings out the natural sweetness in vegetables.
   - Sautéing: Quick and easy method for cooking proteins and vegetables.
   - Blending: Ideal for making smoothies, sauces, and soups.

Tips and Tricks:

1. **Staying Hydrated**

Hydration is crucial on a keto diet as it helps with digestion and prevents the "keto flu." Aim to drink plenty of water and consider electrolyte supplements to balance sodium, potassium, and magnesium levels.

2. **Smart Snacking**

Having keto-friendly snacks on hand can prevent you from reaching for carb-laden options:

   - Cheese and Nuts: Quick and easy to grab.
   - Hard-boiled eggs: Pre-cooked and ready to eat.
   - Avocado Slices: Healthy fat-packed snack.
   - Olives: Flavorful and convenient.

3. **Reading Nutrition Labels**

Learn to read nutrition labels to avoid hidden carbs and sugars:

   - Total Carbs vs. Net Carbs: Subtract fiber and sugar alcohols from total carbs to get net carbs.
   - Ingredient Lists: Look out for added sugars and starches.

4. **Dining Out and Socializing: Staying Keto-Friendly**

Dining out and social gatherings can be tricky, but with some planning, you can stay on track:

   - Research Menus: Look for keto-friendly options at restaurants.
   - Communicate Your Needs: Don't hesitate to ask for modifications.
   - Bring Your Food: Bring a keto-friendly dish to share for gatherings.

Utilizing these techniques, tips, and tricks can make the transition to a keto lifestyle smoother and more sustainable. The keto diet offers numerous health benefits and allows you to enjoy delicious and satisfying meals while achieving your health goals.

What to Eat and Avoid

The key to success on the keto diet lies in making smart food choices. Here's a guide to help you navigate what to include and what to avoid in your keto meals:

What to Eat:

Healthy Fats:

Healthy fats are the cornerstone of the keto diet. They provide the primary source of energy and help maintain ketosis. Focus on incorporating the following fats into your diet:

- **Avocados:** Rich in monounsaturated fats.
- **Olive Oil:** A staple for cooking and dressings.
- **Coconut Oil:** High in medium-chain triglycerides (MCTs).
- **Butter and Ghee:** Opt for grass-fed varieties.
- **Nuts and Seeds:** Almonds, chia seeds, and flaxseeds.

Proteins:

Proteins should be consumed in moderation to prevent disrupting ketosis. Prioritize high-quality protein sources:

- **Meat:** Beef, pork, lamb, and poultry.
- **Fish and Seafood:** Salmon, mackerel, sardines, and shellfish.
- **Eggs:** A versatile and nutrient-dense option.
- **Dairy:** Cheese, yogurt, and heavy cream (preferably full-fat and grass-fed).

Low-Carb Vegetables:

Non-starchy vegetables are essential for providing vitamins, minerals, and fiber while keeping carb intake low:

- **Leafy Greens:** Spinach, kale, and arugula.
- **Cruciferous Vegetables:** Broccoli, cauliflower, and Brussels sprouts.
- **Zucchini and Squash:** Great for adding volume to meals.
- **Peppers and Onions:** Use sparingly to add flavor.

Low-Carb Fruits:

While most fruits are high in carbs, some can be enjoyed in moderation:

- **Berries:** Strawberries, blueberries, raspberries, and blackberries.

What to Avoid:

To stay in ketosis, it's crucial to avoid foods high in carbohydrates:

- **Sugary Foods:** Candy, soda, pastries, and desserts.
- **Grains and Starches:** Bread, pasta, rice, and cereals.
- **High-carb fruits:** Bananas, apples, grapes, and oranges.
- **Legumes:** Beans, lentils, and chickpeas.
- **Processed Foods:** Avoid foods with hidden sugars and unhealthy fats.

By focusing on high-fat, moderate-protein, and low-carb foods, you can successfully maintain ketosis and enjoy the benefits of the keto diet.

Embracing the Keto Lifestyle

• **Holistic Approach**: Incorporate regular exercise, adequate sleep, and stress management into your routine. These factors complement the diet and contribute to overall well-being.

• **Enjoy the Process:** Experiment with new recipes and flavors. The keto diet offers a vast range of delicious options that can be both enjoyable and satisfying.

The Ketogenic diet is more than just a way of eating—it's a lifestyle that can yield significant health benefits and overall well-being. By incorporating these practical techniques, tips, and tricks, you can maximize your success and enjoyment on the keto journey. Remember, the key to sustainability is finding a balance that works for you, making informed choices, and staying motivated. Embrace the process with enthusiasm, and celebrate the positive.

CHAPTER 3

Keto Breakfasts

1. Avocado and Bacon Breakfast Bowl

2 Servings   **25 Minutes**

INGREDIENTS:

• 4 slices bacon (120 g)
• 2 large eggs (100 g)
• 1 large avocado (200 g)
• 1 cup baby spinach (30 g)
• 40 g cup cherry tomatoes, halved
• 2 tablespoons olive oil (30 ml)
• 1 tablespoon butter (14 g)
• Salt and pepper for taste

INSTRUCTIONS:

1. Heat a frying pan over medium heat.

• Add bacon slices and cook until crisp, about 4 to 5 minutes per side.

• Remove and cut into small pieces.

2. In the same skillet, remove excess bacon fat, reserving about 1 tablespoon.Add the butter and cook the eggs, sunny side up, until the whites are set, about 3 to 4 minutes. Season with salt and pepper.

3. Cut the avocado in half, remove the pit and place in a bowl.

4 .Divide the avocado into two bowls.

• Top with 1/2 cup spinach, 1/4 cup cherry tomatoes, boiled egg and chopped bacon.

• Drizzle with olive oil.

Nutritional Information (per 100 grams): **Calories:** 198 kcal • **Protein:** 7,3g • **Carbs:** 3,2g • **Fats:** 17,8g • **Fiber:** 2,6g

2. Keto Spinach and Feta Omelette

1 Servings   **15 Minutes**

INGREDIENTS:

• 3 large eggs (150g)
• 1/4 cup crumbled feta cheese (30g)
• 1 cup fresh spinach, roughly chopped (30g)
• 1 tbsp butter (14g)
• 1 tbsp heavy cream (15ml)
• Salt and pepper, to taste

INSTRUCTIONS:

1. Prepare the Ingredients:

• Beat the eggs with heavy cream, salt, and pepper.

2. Cook the Spinach:

• Heat a non-stick skillet over medium heat.

• Add butter and sauté spinach until wilted, about 1-2 minutes.

3. Cook the Omelette:

• Pour the eggs into the skillet and cook until edges set, about 2-3 minutes.

• Sprinkle feta over one half and fold the omelet.

• Cook for another 1-2 minutes until set.

Nutritional Information (per 100 grams): **Calories:** 171 kcal • **Protein:** 11,1g • **Carbs:** 2,2g • **Fats:** 13,5g • **Fiber:** 0,6g

3. Cauliflower Hash Browns

🍴 4 Servings   🕐 35 Minutes

Cooking Tips:
- Ensure the cauliflower is dry before mixing.
- Use a non-stick skillet for easier cooking.

INGREDIENTS:

- 3 cups grated cauliflower (300g)
- 2 large eggs (100g)
- 1/2 cup shredded cheddar cheese (50g)
- 1/4 cup almond flour (28g)
- 1 tsp garlic powder (3g)
- Salt and pepper, to taste
- 2 tbsp olive oil (30ml)

INSTRUCTIONS:

1. Prepare the Mixture:

- Mix cauliflower, eggs, cheese, almond flour, garlic powder, salt, and pepper.

2. Form the Hash Browns:

- Shape the mixture into patties.

3. Cook the Hash Browns:

- Heat olive oil in a skillet over medium heat.

- Cook patties until golden brown, about 4-5 minutes per side.

Nutritional Information (per 100 grams): **Calories:** 150 kcal • **Protein:** 7,2g • **Carbs:** 3,5g • **Fats:** 12,3g • **Fiber:** 1,8g

4. Egg and Cheese Breakfast Muffins

🍴 6 Servings   🕐 35 Minutes

Cooking Tips:
- Add cooked bacon or sausage for extra protein.
- Use silicone muffin cups for easy removal

INGREDIENTS:

- 6 large eggs (300g)
- /2 cup shredded mozzarella cheese (56g)
- 1/4 cup diced bell peppers (30g)
- 1/4 cup chopped spinach (30g)
- Salt and pepper, to taste
- 1 tbsp olive oil (15ml)

INSTRUCTIONS:

1. Prepare the Mixture:

- Beat eggs, add cheese, bell peppers, spinach, salt, and pepper.

2. Fill the Muffin Tin:

- Grease the muffin tin with olive oil.

- Pour the mixture into the tin, filling each cup about 3/4 full.

3. Bake:

- Preheat oven to 375°F (190°C).

- Bake for 20 minutes until set.

Nutritional Information (per 100 grams): **Calories:** 154 kcal • **Protein:** 10,8g • **Carbs:** 1,6g • **Fats:** 11,8g • **Fiber:** 0,4g

5. Chia Seed Pudding with Berries

4 Servings

10 Minutes
(Plus 4 hours or overnight)

Cooking Tips:
• For a creamier texture, blend the pudding after it has thickened.
• Use a variety of berries like strawberries, blueberries, and raspberries for added flavor and color.

INGREDIENTS:

• Chia seeds: 60 grams
• Unsweetened almond milk: 480 ml (480 grams)
• Vanilla extract: 5 ml (4 grams)
• Stevia or erythritol: 5 grams (optional, to taste)
• Fresh mixed berries: 200 grams (for topping)

INSTRUCTIONS:

1. In a medium bowl, combine chia seeds, almond milk, vanilla extract, and sweetener (if using). Stir well.

2. Let the mixture sit for 10 minutes, then stir again to break up any clumps.

3. Cover the bowl and refrigerate for at least 4 hours or overnight until the pudding has thickened.

4. Before serving, stir the pudding again and divide it into 4 portions.

5. Top each portion with 50 grams of fresh mixed berries.

Nutritional Information (per 100 grams): **Calories:** 80 kcal • **Protein:** 2g • **Carbs:** 5g • **Fats:** 5g • **Fiber:** 4g

6. Low-Carb Breakfast Casserole

6 Servings

45 Minutes

Cooking Tips:
• Add different vegetables like bell peppers or mushrooms for variety.
• Make ahead and refrigerate for quick breakfast options during the week.

INGREDIENTS:

• Eggs: 8 large (400 grams)
• Heavy cream: 120 ml (120 grams)
• Cooked bacon, chopped: 200 grams
• Spinach, chopped: 100 grams
• Cheddar cheese, shredded: 150 grams
• Salt: 5 grams
• Black pepper: 3 grams

INSTRUCTIONS:

1. Preheat the oven to 180°C (350°F).

2. Whisk the eggs and heavy cream until well combined in a large bowl.

3. Stir in the chopped bacon, spinach, and half of the shredded cheddar cheese—season with salt and pepper.

4. Pour the mixture into a greased baking dish and sprinkle the remaining cheese on top.

5. Bake for 30-35 minutes until the casserole is set and the top is golden brown.

6. Let it cool slightly before cutting into six portions per side

Nutritional Information (per 100 grams): **Calories:** 150 kcal • **Protein:** 10g • **Carbs:** 2g • **Fats:** 12g • **Fiber:** 0g

7. Keto Pancakes with Butter and Syrup

🍴 **4 Servings**
(8 pancakes)

🕐 **20 Minutes**

Cooking Tips:
• Use a measuring spoon to ensure evenly sized pancakes.
• Serve with fresh berries or a dollop of whipped cream for added flavour.

INSTRUCTIONS:

1. Mix almond flour, coconut flour, and baking powder in a medium bowl.

2. Whisk together eggs, almond milk, vanilla extract, and erythritol in another bowl.

3. Combine the wet and dry ingredients, stirring until smooth.

4. Heat a non-stick skillet over medium heat and melt a small amount of butter.

5. Pour two tablespoons of batter per pancake onto the skillet. Cook until bubbles form on the surface, then flip and cook until golden brown.

6. Serve pancakes with remaining melted butter and sugar-free syrup.

INGREDIENTS:

• Almond flour: 100 grams
• Coconut flour: 20 grams
• Baking powder: 10 grams
• Eggs: 4 large (200 grams)
• Unsweetened almond milk: 120 ml (120 grams)
• Vanilla extract: 5 ml (4 grams)
• Erythritol: 15 grams (optional, to taste)

Nutritional Information (per 100 grams): Calories: 210 kcal • **Protein:** 8g • **Carbs:** 5g • **Fats:** 17g • **Fiber:** 4g

8. Sausage and Egg Breakfast Skillet

🍴 **4 Servings**

🕐 **25 Minutes**

Cooking Tips:
• Use pre-cooked sausage to save time.
• Experiment with different cheeses like feta or mozzarella

INSTRUCTIONS:

1. Heat olive oil in a large skillet over medium heat.

2. Add the sausage and cook until browned, breaking it up with a spatula.

3. Add the diced bell peppers and onions, cooking until they are softened.

4. Stir in the spinach and cook until wilted.

5. Create wells in the mixture and crack an egg into each well.

6. Cover the skillet and cook until eggs are set to your preference.

7. Sprinkle with cheddar cheese, salt, and pepper before serving.

INGREDIENTS:

• Breakfast sausage: 300 grams
• Eggs: 8 large (400 grams)
• Bell peppers, diced: 150 grams
• Onions, diced: 100 grams
• Spinach: 100 grams
• Cheddar cheese, shredded: 100 grams
• Olive oil: 20 ml (20 grams)
• Salt: 5 grams • Black pepper: 3

Nutritional Information (per 100 grams): Calories: 180 kcal • **Protein:** 12g • **Carbs:** 3g • **Fats:** 14g • **Fiber:** 1g

9. Keto French Toast

🍴 🕐
4 Servings   **20 Minutes**

Cooking Tips:
• Use a non-stick skillet to prevent sticking.
• Garnish with fresh berries or a dusting of powdered erythritol for added flavor.

INGREDIENTS:

• Almond flour bread: 8 slices (200 grams)
• Eggs: 4 large (200 grams)
• Heavy cream: 120 ml (120 grams)
• Vanilla extract: 5 ml (4 grams)
• Cinnamon: 2 grams
• Butter: 40 grams (for cooking)
• Sugar-free syrup: 80 ml (80 grams, for serving)

INSTRUCTIONS:

1. Whisk together the eggs, heavy cream, vanilla extract, and cinnamon in a shallow dish.

2. Dip each slice of almond flour bread into the egg mixture, ensuring both sides are well coated.

3. Heat butter in a large skillet over medium heat.

4. Cook the dipped bread slices until golden brown on both sides, about 2-3 minutes per side.

5. Serve with sugar-free syrup

Nutritional Information (per 100 grams): **Calories:** 250 kcal • **Protein:** 8g • **Carbs:** 4g • **Fats:** 22g • **Fiber:** 3g

10. Smoked Salmon and Avocado Eggs Benedict

🍴 🕐
2 Servings   **20 Minutes**

Cooking Tips:
• Ensure the water is at a gentle simmer to achieve perfect poached eggs.
• Use ready-made hollandaise sauce for convenience or make your own for a fresher taste.

INGREDIENTS:

• Eggs: 4 large (200 grams)
• Smoked salmon: 100 grams
• Avocado: 1 medium (150 grams)
• Hollandaise sauce: 60 ml (60 grams)
• Lemon juice: 5 ml (4 grams)
• Salt: 2 grams
• Black pepper: 1 gram
• Fresh dill: 5 grams (for garnish)

INSTRUCTIONS:

1. Halve the avocado and remove the pit. Scoop out the flesh and slice it.

2. Heat water in a saucepan and add a splash of vinegar. Bring to a gentle simmer.

3. Crack the eggs into separate small bowls, then gently slide them into the simmering water. Poach for 3-4 minutes.

4. While the eggs are poaching, divide the smoked salmon and avocado slices between two plates.

5. Place two poached eggs on each plate, then drizzle with hollandaise sauce.

6. Sprinkle with lemon juice, salt, pepper, and fresh dill before serving

Nutritional Information (per 100 grams): **Calories:** 200 kcal • **Protein:** 12g • **Carbs:** 3g • **Fats:** 16g • **Fiber:** 2g

11. Keto Waffles

🍴 **4 Servings**
(8 waffles)

🕐 **20 Minutes**

INSTRUCTIONS:

1. Preheat the waffle iron according to the manufacturer's instructions.

2. Mix almond flour, coconut flour, and baking powder in a medium bowl.

3. Whisk together eggs, almond milk, vanilla extract, and erythritol in another bowl.

4. Combine the wet and dry ingredients, stirring until smooth.

5. Grease the waffle iron with butter and pour the batter onto the waffle plates.

6. Cook according to the waffle iron instructions until golden brown.

7. Serve with sugar-free syrup.

INGREDIENTS:

• Almond flour: 100 grams
• Coconut flour: 20 grams
• Baking powder: 10 grams
• Eggs: 4 large (200 grams)
• Unsweetened almond milk: 120 ml (120 grams)
• Vanilla extract: 5 ml (4 grams)
• Erythritol: 15 grams (optional, to taste)

Nutritional Information (per 100 grams): **Calories:** 210 kcal • **Protein:** 8g • **Carbs:** 5g • **Fats:** 17g • **Fiber:** 4g

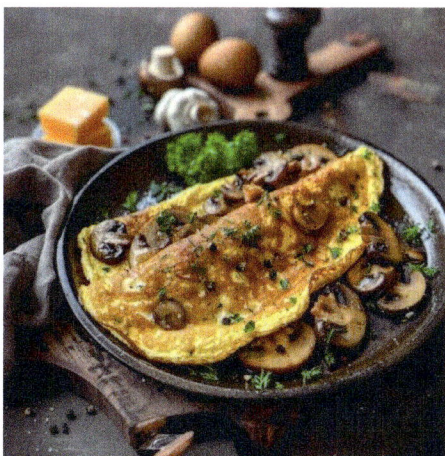

12. Mushroom and Cheese Omelette

🍴 **2 Servings**

🕐 **15 Minutes**

INSTRUCTIONS:

1. Whisk the eggs with salt and pepper in a medium bowl.

2. Heat butter in a non-stick skillet over medium heat.

3. Add the mushrooms and sauté until softened, about 3-4 minutes.

4. Pour the whisked eggs over the mushrooms and cook until the edges start to set.

5. Sprinkle the shredded cheddar cheese over one-half of the omelet.

6. Fold the omelet in half and cook until the cheese is melted and the eggs are fully set.

7. Slide the omelet onto a plate and serve immediately.

INGREDIENTS:

• Eggs: 4 large (200 grams)
• Mushrooms, sliced: 100 grams
• Cheddar cheese, shredded: 60 grams
• Butter: 20 grams
• Salt: 2 grams
• Black pepper: 1 gram

Nutritional Information (per 100 grams): **Calories:** 180 kcal • **Protein:** 11g • **Carbs:** 2g • **Fats:** 14g • **Fiber:** 1g

13. Keto Cinnamon Rolls

🍴 8 Servings   🕐 40 Minutes

INGREDIENTS:

• Mozzarella cheese, shredded: 170 grams
• Cream cheese: 30 grams
• Almond flour: 150 grams
• Coconut flour: 20 grams
• Baking powder: 10 grams
• Eggs: 2 large (100 grams)
• Erythritol: 50 grams
• Ground cinnamon: 10 grams
• Butter, melted: 60 grams
• Vanilla extract: 5 ml (4 grams)

INSTRUCTIONS:

1. Preheat the oven to 180°C (350°F). Line a baking dish with parchment paper.
2. In a microwave-safe bowl, combine mozzarella and cream cheese. Microwave for 1-2 minutes until melted, stirring halfway.
3. Mix almond flour, coconut flour, and baking powder in another bowl.
4. Add the melted cheese mixture to the dry ingredients, eggs, and vanilla extract. Mix until a dough forms.
5. Roll the dough between two sheets of parchment paper into a rectangle about 1/4 inch thick.
6. Brush the dough with melted butter and sprinkle with erythritol and cinnamon.
7. Roll the dough tightly into a log and slice it into eight pieces. Place the rolls in the prepared baking dish.
8. Bake for 20-25 minutes until golden brown. Let cool slightly before serving.

Nutritional Information (per 100 grams): **Calories:** 280 kcal • **Protein:** 10g • **Carbs:** 6g • **Fats:** 24g • **Fiber:** 4g

14. Scrambled Eggs with Cream Cheese

🍴 2 Servings   🕐 10 Minutes

INSTRUCTIONS:

1. In a bowl, whisk the eggs with salt and pepper.
2. Heat butter in a non-stick skillet over medium heat.
3. Pour the eggs into the skillet and cook, stirring gently.
4. When the eggs are partially set, add small dollops of cream cheese.
5. Continue to cook until the eggs are fully set and the cream cheese is melted.
6. Serve immediately.

INGREDIENTS:

• Eggs: 4 large (200 grams)
• Cream cheese: 60 grams
• Butter: 20 grams
• Salt: 2 grams
• Black pepper: 1 gram

Nutritional Information (per 100 grams): **Calories:** 220 kcal • **Protein:** 10g • **Carbs:** 2g • **Fats:** 19g • **Fiber:** 0g

15. Low-Carb Bagels with Cream Cheese

🍴 6 Servings

🕐 35 Minutes

Cooking Tips:
• *Wet your hands to prevent the dough from sticking while shaping the bagels.*
• *Store leftover bagels in the refrigerator and toast before serving.*

INGREDIENTS:

• Almond flour: 150 grams
• Coconut flour: 20 grams
• Baking powder: 10 grams
• Eggs: 2 large (100 grams)
• Mozzarella cheese, shredded: 170 grams
• Cream cheese: 30 grams
• Everything bagel seasoning: 20 grams (optional)
• Cream cheese (for serving): 120 grams

INSTRUCTIONS:

1. Preheat the oven to 190°C (375°F). Line a baking sheet with parchment paper.

2. In a microwave-safe bowl, combine mozzarella and cream cheese. Microwave for 1-2 minutes until melted, stirring halfway.

3. Mix almond flour, coconut flour, and baking powder in another bowl.

4. Add the melted cheese mixture to the dry ingredients and the eggs. Mix until a dough forms.

5. Divide the dough into 6 equal parts and shape each into a bagel.

6. Place the bagels on the prepared baking sheet and sprinkle with everything bagel seasoning, if using.

7. Bake for 20-25 minutes until golden brown. Let cool slightly before serving with cream cheese.

Nutritional Information (per 100 grams): **Calories:** 270 kcal • **Protein:** 12g • **Carbs:** 5g • **Fats:** 22g • **Fiber:** 3g

16. Zucchini Fritters

🍴 4 Servings

🕐 20 Minutes

Cooking Tips:
• *Ensure the zucchini is well-drained to prevent soggy fritters.*
• *Serve with a dollop of sour cream or Greek yogurt for added flavor.*

INSTRUCTIONS:

1. Place the grated zucchini in a clean kitchen towel and squeeze out excess moisture.

2. Combine the zucchini, almond flour, Parmesan cheese, eggs, garlic powder, salt, and pepper in a large bowl. Mix well.

3. Heat olive oil in a skillet over medium heat.

4. Scoop 2 tablespoons of the mixture per patty into the skillet and flatten with a spatula.

5. Cook for 3-4 minutes on each side until golden brown.

6. Drain on paper towels and serve warm.

INGREDIENTS:

• Zucchini, grated: 400 grams
• Almond flour: 60 grams
• Parmesan cheese, grated: 40 grams
• Eggs: 2 large (100 grams)
• Garlic powder: 5 grams
• Salt: 5 grams
• Black pepper: 2 grams
• Olive oil: 30 ml (30 grams) for frying

Nutritional Information (per 100 grams): **Calories:** 150 kcal • **Protein:** 6g • **Carbs:** 4g • **Fats:** 12g • **Fiber:** 2g

17. Keto Breakfast Pizza

🍴 **4 Servings** 🕐 **30 Minutes**

Cooking Tips:
• Ensure the crust is evenly spread for uniform cooking.
• Customize the toppings with your favorite low-carb vegetables or meats.

INGREDIENTS:
• Almond flour: 150 grams
• Mozzarella cheese, shredded: 170 g
• Cream cheese: 30 grams
• Eggs: 4 large (100 grams)
• Baking powder: 5 grams
• Olive oil: 20 ml (20 grams)
• Cooked bacon, crumbled: 100 grams
• Cheddar cheese, shredded: 100 grams
• Green onions, chopped: 20 grams
• Salt: 2 grams

INSTRUCTIONS:
1. Preheat the oven to 200°C (400°F). Line a baking sheet with parchment paper.
2. In a microwave-safe bowl, combine mozzarella and cream cheese. Microwave for 1-2 minutes until melted, stirring halfway.
3. In another bowl, mix almond flour and baking powder.
4. Add the melted cheese mixture to the dry ingredients along with 2 eggs and olive oil. Mix until a dough forms.
5. Spread the dough onto the prepared baking sheet to form a pizza crust.
6. Bake for 10-12 minutes until golden brown.
7. Remove from the oven and top with crumbled bacon, shredded cheddar cheese, and chopped green onions.
8. Crack 4 eggs over the toppings and season with salt and pepper.
9. Return to the oven and bake for 10-12 minutes until the eggs are set.
10. Slice and serve immediately.

Nutritional Information (per 100 grams): **Calories:** 250 kcal • **Protein:** 13g • **Carbs:** 4g • **Fats:** 20g • **Fiber:** 2g

18. Keto Shakshuka

🍴 **4 Servings** 🕐 **30 Minutes**

Cooking Tips:
• Use fresh tomatoes in place of canned for a fresher taste. Adjust spices to taste for more or less heat.

INSTRUCTIONS:
1. Heat olive oil in a large skillet over medium heat. Add the onion and bell pepper, cooking until soft (about 5 minutes).

2. Add garlic, cumin, paprika, and chili powder. Cook for another 1-2 minutes until fragrant.

3. Add the diced tomatoes and water and bring to a simmer. Cook for about 10 minutes until the sauce thickens.

4. Make small wells in the sauce and crack an egg into each well. Cover the skillet and cook for 5-7 minutes until the eggs are set to your liking.

5. Season with salt and pepper, and garnish with fresh parsley if desired.

INGREDIENTS:
• 6 large eggs (300 g), 30 ml olive oil
• 1 large onion, diced (150 g)
• 1 red bell pepper, diced (150 g)
• 3 cloves garlic, minced (9 g)
• 1 tsp paprika •1/2 tsp chili powder
• 1 can (400 g) diced tomatoes (with juice)
• 1/2 cup water (120 ml) • cumin 2 g
• Salt and pepper to taste
• Fresh parsley, chopped (optional, for garnish)

Nutritional Information (per 100 grams): **Calories:** 80 kcal • **Protein:** 4g • **Carbs:** 5g • **Fats:** 5g • **Fiber:** 1g

19. Ham and Cheese Frittata

🍴 **6 Servings**　　🕐 **25 Minutes**

Cooking Tips:
• Add your favorite vegetables like spinach or mushrooms for more flavor and nutrients.

INGREDIENTS:

• 8 large eggs (400 g)
• 1/2 cup heavy cream (120 ml)
• 1 cup diced ham (150 g)
• 1 cup shredded cheddar cheese (100 g)
• 1/2 cup diced green onions (50 g)
• Salt and pepper to taste
• 2 tbsp butter (28 g)

INSTRUCTIONS:

1. Preheat the oven to 375°F (190°C).

2. whisk together the eggs, heavy cream, salt, and pepper in a large bowl.

3. Stir in the ham, cheese, and green onions.

4. Heat the butter in an oven-safe skillet over medium heat. Pour in the egg mixture.

5. Cook on the stove until the edges start to set, then transfer to the oven.

6. Bake for 15-20 minutes until the frittata is fully set and golden brown on top

Nutritional Information (per 100 grams): Calories: 180 kcal • **Protein:** 12g • **Carbs:** 1 g • **Fats:** 15g • **Fiber:** 0g

---

20. Green Eggs and Ham

🍴 **2 Servings**　　🕐 **20 Minutes**

Cooking Tips:
• Substitute kale or arugula for spinach for a different flavor. Add a squeeze of lemon juice for a fresh finish

INSTRUCTIONS:

1. Whisk together the eggs, heavy cream, salt, and pepper in a bowl.

2. Heat the butter in a non-stick skillet over medium heat. Add the spinach and cook until wilted.

3. Stir in the pesto and cook for another 1-2 minutes.

4. Add the eggs and ham, stirring constantly until the eggs are fully cooked.

INGREDIENTS:

• 6 large eggs (300 g)
• 2 tbsp heavy cream (30 ml)
• Salt and pepper to taste
• 1 tbsp butter (14 g)
• 1/2 cup chopped spinach (30 g)
• 1/4 cup basil pesto (60 g)
• 1 cup diced ham (150 g)

Nutritional Information (per 100 grams): Calories: 160 kcal • **Protein:** 10g • **Carbs:** 2g • **Fats:** 13g • **Fiber:** 1g

21. Keto Cottage Cheese Pancakes

4 Servings
(8 Pancakes)

25 Minutes

Cooking Tips:
• *Consistency: If the batter seems too thick, you can add a bit more almond milk until the desired consistency is reached.*

INGREDIENTS:
• 225 grams cottage cheese
• 3 large eggs
• 30 grams almond flour
• 30 grm) coconut flour
• 60 ml unsweetened almond milk
• 15 grams erythritol (optional, for sweetness)
• 5 ml vanilla extract
• 1/2 teaspoon (2.5 grams) baking powder
• 1/4 teaspoon (1.25 grams) salt
• 30 gramsunsalted butter (for cooking)

INSTRUCTIONS:

1. Prepare the Batter:
Combine cottage cheese, eggs, almond flour, coconut flour, almond milk, erythritol (if using), vanilla extract, baking powder, and salt in a medium bowl.Mix until smooth using a blender or an immersion blender for a consistent texture.

2. Heat the Pan:
Preheat a non-stick skillet or griddle over medium heat.
Add 1/2 tablespoon of butter and let it melt and coat the pan.

3. Cook the Pancakes:
Pour about 1/4 cup of the batter onto the skillet for each pancake.
Cook until bubbles form on the surface and the edges start to set, about 2-3 minutes.
Flip the pancakes and cook for 2-3 minutes, until golden brown and cooked through.
Repeat with the remaining batter, adding more butter to the pan as needed.

4. Serve:
Serve warm with keto-friendly toppings such as sugar-free syrup, fresh berries, or a dollop of whipped cream.

Nutritional Information (per 100 grams): **Calories:** 185 kcal • **Protein:** 11g • **Carbs:** 5g • **Fats:** 14g • **Fiber:** 3g

22. Keto Breakfast Rolls

4 Servings

30 Minutes

Cooking Tips:
• *Use a non-stick skillet and butter to prevent sticking and tearing of the egg wraps.*

INGREDIENTS:
• Chicken eggs – 10 pcs
• Cheddar cheese – 150 g
• Fried sausages – 5 pcs
• Bacon slices (fried) – 5 pcs
• Salt and pepper to tast

INSTRUCTIONS:

1. In a bowl, mix two eggs and pour onto a preheated skillet. Season with salt and pepper.

2. Cook under a lid over medium heat for two to three minutes.

3. When the eggs are almost ready, lay out 30 g of cheese, a sausage cut lengthwise, and a bacon slice.

4. Carefully fold the edges of the omelet up to form a roll and flip.5. Cook and remove the ready roll from the skillet.

6. Repeat steps 1-4 five more times.

Nutritional Information (per 100 grams): **Calories:** 251 kcal • **Protein:** 13,44g • **Carbs:** 3,5g • **Fats:** 0,67g • **Fiber:** 0

CHAPTER 4

Keto Salad & Soup

1. Greek Chicken Salad

🍴 **4 Servings**   🕐 **30 Minutes**

Cooking Tips:
• *For more flavor, marinate the chicken breast in olive oil, lemon juice, and oregano before cooking*

INSTRUCTIONS:

1. Combine the chicken, cucumber, cherry tomatoes, red onion, olives, and feta cheese in a large bowl.

2. Whisk together the olive oil, red wine vinegar, oregano, salt, and pepper in a small bowl.3. Pour the dressing over the salad and toss to combine.

4. Serve chilled or at room temperature.

INGREDIENTS:

• 500 g chicken breast, cooked and diced
• 1 large cucumber, diced (300 g)
• 150 g cherry tomatoes, halved
• 1/2 red onion, thinly sliced (50 g)
• 75 g Kalamata olives, sliced
• 100 g feta cheese, crumbled
• 60 ml extra-virgin olive oil
• 2 tbsp red wine vinegar (30 ml)
• 1 tsp dried oreano (1 g)
• Salt and pepper to taste

Nutritional Information (per 100 grams): **Calories:** 140 kcal • **Protein:** 10g • **Carbs:** 3g • **Fats:** 10g • **Fiber:** 1g

2. Keto Cobb Salad

🍴 **4 Servings**   🕐 **20 Minutes**

Cooking Tips:
• *Use homemade ranch dressing to control the ingredients and ensure it's keto-friendly.*

INSTRUCTIONS:

1. Combine the romaine lettuce, eggs, avocado, chicken, bacon, blue cheese, and cherry tomatoes in a large bowl.

2. Drizzle with ranch dressing and toss gently to combine.

3. Serve immediately

INGREDIENTS:

• 200 g romaine lettuce, chopped
• 2 hard-boiled eggs, diced (100 g)
• 1 avocado, diced (200 g)
• 1 cup cooked chicken breast, diced (200 g)
• 50 g slices cooked bacon, crumbled
• 1/2 cup blue cheese, crumbled (75 g)
• 1/2 cup cherry tomatoes, halved (75 g)
• 1/4 cup ranch dressing (60 ml)

Nutritional Information (per 100 grams): **Calories:** 190 kcal • **Protein:** 10g • **Carbs:** 3g • **Fats:** 16g • **Fiber:** 2g

3. Avocado and Bacon Salad

🍴 **2 Servings**

🕐 **15 Minutes**

INGREDIENTS:

• 4 slices bacon (120 g)
• 2 large eggs (100 g)
• 1 large avocado (200 g)
• 1 cup baby spinach (30 g)
• 40 g cup cherry tomatoes, halved
• 2 tablespoons olive oil (30 ml)
• 1 tablespoon butter (14 g)
• Salt and pepper for taste

INSTRUCTIONS:

1. Combine the mixed greens, avocado, bacon, red onion, and cherry tomatoes in a large bowl.

2. Whisk together the olive oil, apple cider vinegar, salt, and pepper in a small bowl.3. Drizzle the dressing over the salad and toss to combine.

4. Serve immediately.

Nutritional Information (per 100 grams): Calories: 160 kcal • Protein: 4g • Carbs: 3g • Fats: 14g • Fiber: 3g

4. Taco Salad with Avocado Dressing

🍴 **4 Servings**

🕐 **20 Minutes**

INGREDIENTS:

• 500 g ground beef
• 1 tbsp taco seasoning (8 g)
• 300 g romaine lettuce, chopped
• 150 G cherry tomatoes, halved
• 1/2 red onion, diced (50 g)
• 50 g shredded cheddar cheese
• 1 avocado, diced (200 g)
• 1/4 cup sour cream (60 g)
• 2 tbsp lime juice (30 ml) •2 tbsp olive oil
• Salt and pepper to taste

INSTRUCTIONS:

1. Cook the ground beef in a skillet over medium heat until browned. Drain excess fat and stir in taco seasoning. Set aside.

2. Combine the lettuce, cherry tomatoes, red onion, and cheddar cheese in a large bowl.

3. For the dressing, blend the avocado, sour cream, lime juice, olive oil, salt, and pepper until smooth.

4. Add the seasoned beef to the salad and drizzle with the avocado dressing.

Nutritional Information (per 100 grams): Calories: 180 kcal • Protein: 10g • Carbs: 3g • Fats: 5g • Fiber: 2g

5. Creamy Cauliflower Soup

🍴 **4 Servings** 🕐 **30 Minutes**

Cooking Tips:
• *Add a pinch of smoked paprika for a different flavor profile. Garnish with fresh herbs like parsley or chives.*

INGREDIENTS:

• 1 head cauliflower, chopped (600 g)
• 1 cup heavy cream (240 ml)
• 2 cups chicken broth (480 ml)
• 1/4 cup grated Parmesan cheese (25 g)
• 1/4 cup chopped onion (40 g)
• 2 cloves garlic, minced (6 g)
• 2 tbsp butter (28 g)
• Salt and pepper to taste
• 1/4 tsp nutmeg (1 g)

INSTRUCTIONS:

1. Melt the butter in a large pot over medium heat. Add the onion and garlic, cooking until softened.

2. Add the cauliflower, heavy cream, and chicken broth. Bring to a boil, then reduce to a simmer and cook until the cauliflower is tender.

3. Use an immersion blender to blend the soup until smooth (or transfer to a blender and blend in batches).

4. Stir in the Parmesan cheese and nutmeg until well combined.

5. Season with salt and pepper to taste and serve warm.

Nutritional Information (per 100 grams): **Calories:** 130 kcal • **Protein:** 3g • **Carbs:** 3g • **Fats:** 11g • **Fiber:** 1g

6. Chicken Zoodle Soup

🍴 **4 Servings** 🕐 **25 Minutes**

Cooking Tips:
• *Add a squeeze of lemon juice for a fresh finish. For a spicier version, add red pepper flakes.*

INGREDIENTS:

• 2 cups cooked chicken breast• chicken broth 960 ml
• Zucchini Noodles (400 g)
• 1 cup chopped celery (100 g)
• 1 cup chopped carrots (120 g)
• 1/4 cup chopped onion (40 g)
• 2 cloves garlic, •2 tbsp olive oil
• 1 tsp dried thyme (1 g)
• 1 tsp dried oregano (1 g)
• Salt and pepper to taste

INSTRUCTIONS:

1. Heat the olive oil in a large pot over medium heat. Add the onion, garlic, celery, and carrots, cooking until softened.

2. Add the broth, shredded chicken, thyme, oregano, salt, and pepper. Bring to a boil, then reduce to a simmer for 10 minutes.

3. Add the zucchini noodles and cook for 3-4 minutes until tender.

4. Serve warm.

Nutritional Information (per 100 grams): **Calories:** 50 kcal • **Protein:** 6g • **Carbs:** 2g • **Fats:** 2g • **Fiber:** 1g

7. Keto Egg Drop Soup

4 Servings   **15 Minutes**

Cooking Tips:
• Stir the soup gently while adding the eggs to ensure smooth, ribbon-like strands

INGREDIENTS:

• 4 cups chicken broth (960 ml)
• 3 large eggs, beaten (150 g)
• 1/4 cup soy sauce or coconut aminos (60 ml)
• 1 tbsp sesame oil (15 ml)
• 1 tbsp cornstarch mixed with 2 tbsp water (optional for thickening)
• 1/4 cup chopped green onions (25 g)
• Salt and pepper to taste

INSTRUCTIONS:

1. Heat chicken broth in a large pot until it simmer.

2. Slowly drizzle the beaten eggs into the broth while stirring to create egg ribbons.

3. Add soy sauce, sesame oil, and, if using, cornstarch mixture to thicken.

4. Season with salt and pepper. Garnish with chopped green onions before serving.

Nutritional Information (per 100 grams): **Calories:** 50 kcal • **Protein:** 4g • **Carbs:** 1g • **Fats:** 3g • **Fiber:** 0g

8. Asian Chicken Salad

4 Servings   **20 Minutes**

Cooking Tips:
• For added crunch, toast the almonds before adding them to the salad.

INSTRUCTIONS:

1. Combine shredded chicken, napa cabbage, carrots, almonds, and green onions in a large bowl.

2. Whisk together sesame oil, rice vinegar, soy sauce, ginger, garlic powder, salt, and pepper in a small bowl.

3. Pour the dressing over the salad and toss to combine.

4. Serve immediately or chill before serving.

INGREDIENTS:

• 300 g cooked chicken breast
• 200 g shredded napa cabbage
• 1 cup shredded carrots (100 g)
• 1/2 cup sliced almonds (50 g)
• 1/4 cup chopped green onions (25 g)
• 1/4 cup sesame oil (60 ml)
• 3 tbsp rice vinegar (45 ml)
• 15 mlvsoy sauce or coconut aminos
• 1 tsp grated ginger
• 1 tsp garlic powder
• Salt and pepper to taste

Nutritional Information (per 100 grams): **Calories:** 150 kcal • **Protein:** 8g • **Carbs:** 5g • **Fats:** 11g • **Fiber:** 2g

9. Creamy Mushroom Soup

4 Servings **30 Minutes**

Cooking Tips:
• *For extra richness, add a splash of sherry or a few tablespoons of cream cheese.*

INGREDIENTS:

• 500 g mushrooms, sliced
• 1 cup heavy cream (240 ml)
• 2 cups chicken broth (480 ml)
• 1/4 cup chopped onion (40 g)
• 2 cloves garlic, minced (6 g)
• 2 tbsp butter (28 g)
• 1/4 cup grated Parmesan cheese (25 g)
• 1 tsp dried thyme (1 g)
• Salt and pepper to taste

INSTRUCTIONS:

1. Melt the butter in a large pot over medium heat. Add the onion and garlic, cooking until softened.

2. Add the mushrooms and cook until they release their juices and start to brown.

3. Pour in the chicken broth and dried thyme. Bring to a boil, then reduce heat and simmer for 10 minutes.

4. Blend the soup until smooth using an immersion blender (or transfer it to a blender and blend in batches).

5. Stir in the heavy cream and Parmesan cheese. Heat through, then season with salt and pepper.

6. Serve warm.

Nutritional Information (per 100 grams): Calories: 120 kcal • **Protein:** 4g • **Carbs:** 5g • **Fats:** 9g • **Fiber:** 1g

10. Shrimp and Avocado Salad

4 Servings **15 Minutes**

Cooking Tips:
• *For extra flavor, add a pinch of smoked paprika or a dash of hot sauce to the shrimp.*

INGREDIENTS:

• 500 g shrimp, peeled and deveined
• 2 avocados, diced (300 g)
• 4 cups mixed greens (120 g)
• 1/2 cup cherry tomatoes, halved (75 g)
• 1/4 cup red onion, thinly sliced (25 g)
• 2 tbsp olive oil (30 ml)
• 1 tbsp lemon juice (15 ml)
• 1 clove garlic, minced (3 g)
• Salt and pepper to taste

INSTRUCTIONS:

1. Heat olive oil in a skillet over medium heat. Add shrimp and garlic, cooking until shrimp are pink and opaque.

2. Combine mixed greens, avocado, cherry tomatoes, and red onion in a large bowl.

3. Drizzle with lemon juice and toss gently.

4. Top with cooked shrimp and season with salt and pepper.

Nutritional Information (per 100 grams): Calories: 180 kcal • **Protein:** 10g • **Carbs:** 6g • **Fats:** 14g • **Fiber:** 5g

CHAPTER 5
Poultry Recipes

1. Garlic Butter Chicken Thighs

4 Servings **30 Minutes**

Cooking Tips:
• For crispy skin, broil the chicken for the last 5 minutes of baking

INSTRUCTIONS:

1. Preheat oven to 375°F (190°C).

2. Season chicken thighs with salt and pepper.

3. Melt butter in a skillet over medium heat. Add minced garlic and cook for 1 minute until fragrant.

4. Transfer the chicken thighs to a baking dish and pour garlic butter.

5. Sprinkle dried rosemary and thyme on top.

6. Bake for 25-30 minutes until the internal temperature reaches 165°F (74°C).

INGREDIENTS:

• 8 chicken thighs, bone-in, skin-on (1 kg)
• 4 tbsp butter (56 g)
• 4 cloves garlic, minced (12 g)
• 1 tsp dried rosemary (1 g)
• 1 tsp dried thyme (1 g)
• Salt and pepper to taste

Nutritional Information (per 100 grams): **Calories:** 220 kcal • **Protein:** 18g • **Carbs:** 0g • **Fats:** 16g • **Fiber:** 0g

2. Keto Chicken Alfredo

4 Servings **25 Minutes**

Cooking Tips:
• To thicken the sauce further, let it simmer a bit longer or add a bit more Parmesan cheese.

INSTRUCTIONS:

1. Heat olive oil in a skillet over medium heat. Add chicken until golden and cooked through, about 7-8 minutes.

2. Remove chicken from the skillet and set aside.

3. Add garlic to the same skillet and cook for 1 minute. Pour in heavy cream and bring to a simmer.

4. Stir in Parmesan cheese until melted and smooth.

5. Return chicken to the skillet and coat with the Alfredo sauce.

6. Season with Italian seasoning, salt, and pepper. Serve warm.

INGREDIENTS:

• 500 g chicken breast
• 1 tbsp olive oil (15 ml)
• 2 cups heavy cream (480 ml)
• 1 cup grated Parmesan cheese (100 g)
• 2 cloves garlic, minced (6 g)
• 1 tsp dried Italian seasoning (1 g)
• Salt and pepper to taste

Nutritional Information (per 100 grams): **Calories:** 280 kcal • **Protein:** 15g • **Carbs:** 3g • **Fats:** 22g • **Fiber:** 0g

3. Buffalo Chicken Wings

🍴 **4 Servings**   🕐 **40 Minutes**

Cooking Tips:
• For extra crispiness, pat the wings dry before tossing with olive oil

INGREDIENTS:

• 1 kg chicken wings
• 2 tbsp olive oil (30 ml)
• 1/2 cup hot sauce (120 ml)
• 2 tbsp unsalted butter (28 g)
• 1/2 tsp garlic powder (1 g)
• 1/2 tsp onion powder (1 g)
• Salt and pepper to taste

INSTRUCTIONS:

1. Preheat oven to 400°F (200°C).

2. Toss chicken wings with olive oil, salt, and pepper. Spread on a baking sheet.

3. Bake for 30-35 minutes, flipping halfway through, until crispy and cooked through. 4. While wings are baking, melt butter in a saucepan over medium heat. Stir in hot sauce, garlic powder, and onion powder.

5. Toss the cooked wings in the buffalo sauce and serve.

Nutritional Information (per 100 grams): **Calories:** 220 kcal • **Protein:** 16g • **Carbs:** 2g • **Fats:** 17g • **Fiber:** 0g

---

4. Keto Chicken Parmesan

🍴 **4 Servings**   🕐 **30 Minutes**

Cooking Tips:
• For a crispier crust, broil the chicken for the last 2-3 minutes of baking

INGREDIENTS:

• 4 boneless, skinless chicken breasts (600 g)
• 1 cup almond flour (96 g)
• 100 g grated Parmesan cheese
•1 large egg, beaten (50 g)
• 240 ml marinara sauce
• 1 cup mozzarella cheese (112 g)
• 1 tsp dried oregano (1 g)
• 1 tsp garlic powder (2 g)
Salt and pepper to taste
• 2 tbsp olive oil (30 ml)

INSTRUCTIONS:

1. Preheat oven to 375°F (190°C). Grease a baking dish with olive oil.

2. Mix almond flour, Parmesan cheese, garlic powder, salt, and pepper in a bowl.

3. Dip each chicken breast in the beaten egg, then coat with the almond flour.

4. Heat olive oil in a skillet over medium heat. Sear chicken breasts for 2-3 minutes on each side until golden brown.

5. Transfer chicken breasts to the baking dish. Top with marinara sauce and shredded mozzarella cheese.

6. Bake for 20-25 minutes until the chicken reaches an internal temperature of 165°F (74°C).

Nutritional Information (per 100 grams): **Calories:** 250 kcal • **Protein:** 22g • **Carbs:** 4g • **Fats:** 16g • **Fiber:** 1g

---

5. Bacon-Wrapped Chicken Breast

4 Servings   **40 Minutes**

INGREDIENTS:

• 4 boneless, skinless chicken breasts (600 g)
• 8 slices bacon (200 g)
• 2 tbsp olive oil (30 ml)
• 1 tsp smoked paprika (1 g)
• 1 tsp garlic powder (2 g)
• Salt and pepper to taste

INSTRUCTIONS:

1. Preheat oven to 400°F (200°C). Grease a baking sheet with olive oil.

2. Season chicken breasts with smoked paprika, garlic powder, salt, and pepper.

3. Wrap each chicken breast with 2 slices of bacon and secure with toothpicks.

4. Place wrapped chicken breasts on the prepared baking sheet.

5. Bake for 35-40 minutes until the chicken reaches an internal temperature of 165°F (74°C) and bacon is crispy.

Nutritional Information (per 100 grams): **Calories:** 290 kcal • **Protein:** 25g • **Carbs:** 1g • **Fats:** 21g • **Fiber:** 0g

6. Keto Chicken Tikka Masala

45 Servings   **45 Minutes**

INGREDIENTS:

• 500 g chicken breast, cut into chunks
• 2 tbsp olive oil (30 ml)
• 1 cup plain Greek yogurt (240 ml)
• 2 tbsp tikka masala spice mix (12 g)
• 1 cup heavy cream (240 ml)
• 1/2 cup tomato puree (120 ml)
• 1 clove garlic, minced (3 g)
• 1 tsp grated ginger (2 g)
• 1/2 tsp cayenne pepper (optional) (0.5 g)
• Salt and pepper to taste

INSTRUCTIONS:

1. Marinate chicken chunks in Greek yogurt and tikka masala spice mix for at least 30 minutes.

2. Heat olive oil in a skillet over medium heat. Add chicken and cook until browned on all sides, about 5-7 min Ute.

3. Add garlic and ginger, cooking for 1 minute. Stir in tomato puree and heavy cream.

4. Simmer for 15 minutes until the chicken is cooked and the sauce thickens. Adjust seasoning with salt, pepper, and cayenne pepper if desired.

Nutritional Information (per 100 grams): **Calories:** 290 kcal • **Protein:** 22g • **Carbs:** 7g • **Fats:** 20g • **Fiber:** 2g

7. Stuffed Chicken Breast with Spinach and Cheese

🍴 **4 Servings**   🕐 **40 Minutes**

Cooking Tips:
• *Ensure the chicken is sealed tightly around the stuffing to prevent leakage during baking.*

INGREDIENTS:

• 4 boneless, skinless chicken breasts (600 g)
• 1 cup fresh spinach, chopped (30 g)
• 1/2 cup cream cheese (120 g)
• 1/2 cup shredded mozzarella cheese (56 g)
• 1 tbsp olive oil (15 ml)
• 1 tsp garlic powder (2 g)
• 1 tsp dried oregano (1 g)
• Salt and pepper to taste

INSTRUCTIONS:

1. Preheat oven to 375°F (190°C). Grease a baking dish.

2. Mix spinach, cream cheese, and mozzarella in a bowl.

3. Cut the chicken breast in half without cutting all the way through and stuff with the spinach mixture. Secure with toothpicks if necessary.Rub chicken breasts with olive oil, garlic powder, oregano, salt, and pepper.

4. Place chicken in the baking dish and bake for 30-35 minutes, or until the internal temperature reaches 165°F (74°C).

Nutritional Information (per 100 grams): **Calories:** 250 kcal • **Protein:** 23g • **Carbs:** 3g • **Fats:** 17g • **Fiber:** 1g

8. Chicken Zucchini Boats

🍴 **4 Servings**   🕐 **35 Minutes**

Cooking Tips:
• *If zucchinis are too watery, pat them dry with a paper towel before filling to prevent a soggy dish.*

INGREDIENTS:

• 2 large zucchinis (400 g)
• 500 g ground chicken
• 1/2 cup shredded cheddar cheese (56 g)
• 1/2 cup marinara sauce (120 ml, unsweetened)
• 1/2 cup diced bell peppers (75 g)
• 1/4 cup diced onion (30 g)
• 2 cloves garlic, minced (6 g)
• 1 tbsp olive oil (15 ml)
• 1 tsp dried basil (1 g)
• Salt and pepper to taste

INSTRUCTIONS:

1. Preheat oven to 375°F (190°C). Slice zucchinis in half lengthwise and scoop out the center to create boats.

2. Heat olive oil in a skillet over medium heat. Add onions, bell peppers, and garlic. Cook until softened.

3. Add ground chicken to the skillet and cook until browned. Stir in marinara sauce and dried basil. Season with salt and pepper.

4. Fill zucchini boats with the chicken mixture and top with shredded cheddar cheese.

5. Place the stuffed zucchinis on a baking sheet and bake for 20-25 minutes, until the zucchinis are tender and the cheese is melted.

Nutritional Information (per 100 grams): **Calories:** 160 kcal • **Protein:** 17g • **Carbs:** 5g • **Fats:** 8g • **Fiber:** 1g

9. Keto BBQ Chicken

4 Servings   **35 Minutes**

Cooking Tips:
• For added flavor, marinate the chicken in BBQ sauce for a few hours before cooking

INSTRUCTIONS:

1. Preheat oven to 375°F (190°C). Grease a baking dish with olive oil.

2. Rub chicken thighs with smoked paprika, garlic powder, salt, and pepper.

3. Heat olive oil in a skillet over medium heat. Sear chicken thighs for 2-3 minutes per side until golden brown.

4. Transfer chicken to the baking dish. Brush with sugar-free BBQ sauce.

5. Bake for 25-30 minutes until chicken reaches an internal temperature of 165°F (74°C).

INGREDIENTS:

• 4 boneless, skinless chicken thighs (600 g)
• 1/2 cup sugar-free BBQ sauce (120 ml)
• 2 tbsp olive oil (30 ml)
• 1 tsp smoked paprika (1 g)
• 1/2 tsp garlic powder (1 g)
• Salt and pepper to taste

Nutritional Information (per 100 grams): **Calories:** 220 kcal • **Protein:** 22g • **Carbs:** 4g • **Fats:** 14g • **Fiber:** 0g

10. Herb Roasted Turkey Breast

6 Servings   **1 Hour**

Cooking Tips:
• Baste the turkey with its own juices halfway through roasting for extra moisture and flavor.

INSTRUCTIONS:

1. Preheat oven to 375°F (190°C). Place a rack in a roasting pan.

2. Rub turkey breast with olive oil, rosemary, thyme, garlic powder, salt, and pepper.

3. Roast in the oven for about 1 hour until the internal temperature reaches 165°F (74°C) and the skin is crispy.

4. Let rest for 10 minutes before slicing.

INGREDIENTS:

• 1.5 kg turkey breast (bone-in, skin-on)
• 2 tbsp olive oil (30 ml)
• 2 tsp dried rosemary (2 g)
• 2 tsp dried thyme (2 g)
• 1 tsp garlic powder (2 g)
• Salt and pepper to taste

Nutritional Information (per 100 grams): **Calories:** 180 kcal • **Protein:** 26g • **Carbs:** 0g • **Fats:** 8g • **Fiber:** 0g

11. Chicken Bacon Ranch Skillet

4 Servings

30 Minutes

INGREDIENTS:

• 500 g chicken breast, cubed
• 6 slices bacon (200 g)
• 1 cup shredded cheddar cheese (112 g)
• 1/2 cup ranch dressing (120 ml, sugar-free)
• 1 cup baby spinach (30 g)
• 1 tbsp olive oil (15 ml)
• 1 tsp garlic powder (2 g)
• Salt and pepper to taste

INSTRUCTIONS:

1. Cook bacon in a skillet over medium heat until crispy. Remove bacon and crumble. Drain excess fat.

2. In the same skillet, heat olive oil. Add chicken, garlic powder, salt, and pepper. Cook until chicken is browned and cooked through.

3. Stir in ranch dressing and baby spinach. Cook until spinach is wilted.

4. Sprinkle shredded cheddar cheese and crumbled bacon over the top. Cover and cook until cheese is melted.

Nutritional Information (per 100 grams): **Calories:** 290 kcal • **Protein:** 22g • **Carbs:** 4g • **Fats:** 20g • **Fiber:** 1g

12. Keto Orange Chicken

4 Servings

30 Minutes

INGREDIENTS:

• 500 g chicken breast, cubed
• 1/4 cup orange zest (30 g)
• 1/4 cup coconut aminos (60 ml)
• 2 tbsp olive oil (30 ml)
• 2 tbsp erythritol or other keto sweetener (24 g)
• 1 tbsp rice vinegar (15 ml)
• 2 cloves garlic, minced (6 g)
• 1 tsp grated ginger (2 g)
• Salt and pepper to taste

INSTRUCTIONS:

1. Heat olive oil in a skillet over medium heat. Add chicken and cook until golden brown and cooked through.

2. In a bowl, mix orange zest, coconut aminos, erythritol, rice vinegar, garlic, and ginger.

3. Pour the orange mixture over the chicken and cook for an additional 5 minutes until the sauce thickens.

4. Season with salt and pepper.

Nutritional Information (per 100 grams): **Calories:** 220 kcal • **Protein:** 22g • **Carbs:** 6g • **Fats:** 12g • **Fiber:** 1g

13. Keto Chicken Teriyaki

4 Servings   **25 Minutes**

Cooking Tips:
• For a thicker sauce, increase the amount of cornstarch or reduce the sauce over low heat.

INGREDIENTS:

•450 g boneless, skinless chicken thighs, cut into bite-sized pieces
•60 ml cup tamari •2 tbsp erythritol (24 g)
•15 ml rice vinegar •15 ml sesame oil
•2 cloves garlic, minced (6 g)
•1 tsp ginger, grated (2 g)
•1/2 cup water (120 ml)
 8 g cornstarch (optional, for thickening)
•1 tbsp sesame seeds (8 g)
•2 green onions, sliced (20 g

INSTRUCTIONS:

1. Mix tamari, erythritol, rice vinegar, sesame oil, garlic, ginger, and water in a bowl.

2. Heat a large skillet over medium-high heat. Add chicken until browned and cooked through, about 7-10 minutes.

3. Pour sauce over chicken and simmer for 5 minutes. Dissolve cornstarch in 2 tbsp water and add to the sauce if thickening is desired.

4. Cook for 2-3 minutes until the sauce has thickened. Garnish with sesame seeds and green onions.

Nutritional Information (per 100 grams): **Calories:** 150 kcal • **Protein:** 20g • **Carbs:** 3g • **Fats:** 7g • **Fiber:** 0,5g

14. Keto Kung Pao Chicken

4 Servings   **20 Minutes**

Cooking Tips:
• Adjust the amount of chili paste based on your heat preference. Toasting the peanuts beforehand adds extra flavor.

INSTRUCTIONS:

1. Heat olive oil in a skillet over medium-high heat.

2. Add chicken and cook until browned and cooked through.

3. Add garlic, bell peppers, and onions. Stir-fry for 3-4 minutes.

4. Mix soy sauce, rice vinegar, erythritol, chili paste, and chicken broth in a bowl.

5. Pour the sauce over the chicken and vegetables. Cook for another 3 minutes.

6. Stir in roasted peanuts before serving.

INGREDIENTS:

•1 lb (450 g) chicken breast, diced
•2 tbsp (30 ml) olive oil
•1/2 cup (75 g) chopped bell peppers
•1/4 cup (30 g) chopped onions
•1/4 cup (30 g) roasted peanuts
•3 cloves garlic, minced (9 g)
•1 tbsp (15 ml) soy sauce or tamari
•2 tbsp (30 ml) rice vinegar
•1 tbsp (15 g) erythritol
•1 tbsp (10 g) chili paste
•1/4 cup (60 ml) chicken broth

Nutritional Information (per 100 grams): **Calories:** 180 kcal • **Protein:** 17g • **Carbs:** 7g • **Fats:** 10g • **Fiber:** 2g

CHAPTER 6

Pork Recipes

1. Garlic Butter Pork Chops

4 Servings   **20 Minutes**

INGREDIENTS:

- 4 bone-in pork chops (600 g)
- 4 tbsp butter (56 g)
- 4 cloves garlic, minced (12 g)
- 1 tbsp olive oil (15 ml)
- 1 tsp dried thyme (1 g)
- 1 tsp dried rosemary (1 g)
- Salt and pepper to taste

INSTRUCTIONS:

1. Heat olive oil in a skillet over medium-high heat.

2. Season pork chops with salt, pepper, thyme, and rosemary.

3. Sear pork chops for 4-5 minutes per side, until golden brown and cooked through. Remove and set aside.

4. In the same skillet, melt butter and add minced garlic. Sauté for 1 minute.

5. Return pork chops to the skillet, spooning garlic butter over them. Serve warm.

Nutritional Information (per 100 grams): **Calories:** 250 kcal • **Protein:** 22g • **Carbs:** 0g • **Fats:** 17g • **Fiber:** 0g

2. Keto Pulled Pork

6 Serving   **6 hours (slow cooker) or 2 hours (Instant Pot)**

INGREDIENTS:

- 1.5 kg pork shoulder
- 1/2 cup apple cider vinegar (120 ml)
- 1/4 cup tomato paste (60 g)
- 1/4 cup keto barbecue sauce (60 ml)
- 1 tbsp smoked paprika (6 g)
- 1 tbsp garlic powder (6 g)
- 1 tbsp onion powder (6 g)
- 1 tsp salt (5 g)
- 1 tsp black pepper (2 g)

INSTRUCTIONS:

1. Combine apple cider vinegar, tomato paste, barbecue sauce, smoked paprika, garlic powder, onion powder, salt, and pepper.

2. Rub mixture all over the pork shoulder.

3. Place pork in a slow cooker and cook on low for 6-8 hours, or until tender. Alternatively, cook in an Instant Pot on high pressure for 60 minutes.

4. Shred pork with forks and mix with cooking juices. Serve warm.

Nutritional Information (per 100 grams): **Calories:** 210 kcal • **Protein:** 22g • **Carbs:** 5g • **Fats:** 12g • **Fiber:** 1g

3. Keto Pork Schnitzel

🍴 🕐

4 Servings   **25 Minutes**

Cooking Tips:
• For extra crispiness, ensure the oil is hot before adding the pork chops.

INGREDIENTS:

• 4 pork loin chops (600 g), pounded thin
• 1/2 cup almond flour (56 g)
• 1/2 cup grated Parmesan cheese (50 g)
• 2 large eggs (100 g), beaten
• 1/4 cup olive oil (60 ml)
• Salt and pepper to taste

INSTRUCTIONS:

1. Mix almond flour and Parmesan cheese in a shallow bowl.

2. Season pork chops with salt and pepper. Dip each chop in beaten eggs, then coat with the almond flour.

3. Heat olive oil in a skillet over medium-high heat. Cook pork chops for 4-5 minutes per side, until golden brown and cooked through.

4. Drain on paper towels before serving.

Nutritional Information (per 100 grams): **Calories:** 290 kcal • **Protein:** 22g • **Carbs:** 3g • **Fats:** 20g • **Fiber:** 2g

4. Keto BBQ Ribs

🍴 🕐

4 Servings   **2,5 Hours**

Cooking Tips:
• For more tender ribs, cook them slowly at a low temperature and make sure to cover with foil during the baking process to retain moisture.

INGREDIENTS:

• 1.5 kg pork ribs
• 1/2 cup sugar-free BBQ sauce (120 ml)
• 2 tbsp smoked paprika (12 g)
• 2 tbsp olive oil (30 ml)
• 1 tbsp garlic powder (9 g)
• 1 tbsp onion powder (9 g)
• 1 tsp salt (5 g)
• 1 tsp black pepper (2 g)

INSTRUCTIONS:

1. Preheat oven to 300°F (150°C). Line a baking sheet with foil and place a rack on top.

2. Remove the membrane from the ribs if needed. Rub the ribs with smoked paprika, garlic powder, onion powder, salt, and pepper.

3. Place ribs on the rack and brush with olive oil. Bake for 2 hours.

4. Remove ribs from oven, brush with sugar-free BBQ sauce, and return to the oven for an additional 30 minutes.

5. Optionally, broil for 5 minutes to caramelize the BBQ sauce.

Nutritional Information (per 100 grams): **Calories:** 220 kcal • **Protein:** 22g • **Carbs:** 5g • **Fats:** 13g • **Fiber:** 0g

5. Bacon-Wrapped Pork Loin

🍴 4 Servings　　🕐 45 Minutes

INSTRUCTIONS:

1. Preheat oven to 375°F (190°C). Line a baking sheet with parchment paper.

2. Rub pork loin with olive oil, rosemary, thyme, garlic powder, salt, and pepper.

3. Wrap pork loin with bacon slices, securing with toothpicks if needed. Place on the baking sheet.

4. Bake for 30-35 minutes or until the internal temperature reaches 145°F (63°C) and bacon is crispy.

5. Let rest for 10 minutes before slicing.

INGREDIENTS:

• 500 g pork loin
• 8 slices bacon (240 g)
• 2 tbsp olive oil (30 ml)
• 1 tsp dried rosemary (1 g)
• 1 tsp dried thyme (1 g)
• 1 tsp garlic powder (2 g)
• Salt and pepper to taste

Nutritional Information (per 100 grams): **Calories:** 300 kcal • **Protein:** 22g • **Carbs:** 0g • **Fats:** 22g • **Fiber:** 0g

6. Italian Sausage and Peppers

🍴 4 Servings　　🕐 30 Minutes

INSTRUCTIONS:

1. Heat olive oil in a skillet over medium heat. Add sausage and cook until browned and cooked through. Remove and slice into pieces.

2. Add garlic, onions, and bell peppers in the same skillet. Cook until vegetables are tender.

3. Return sausage to the skillet, add oregano, basil, salt, and pepper. Stir and cook for another 5 minutes.

INGREDIENTS:

• 500 g Italian sausage (bulk, not links)
• 2 cups sliced bell peppers (240 g)
• 1 cup sliced onions (120 g)
• 2 tbsp olive oil (30 ml)
• 2 cloves garlic, minced (6 g)
• 1/2 tsp dried oregano (1 g)
• 1/2 tsp dried basil (1 g)
• Salt and pepper to taste

Nutritional Information (per 100 grams): **Calories:** 240 kcal • **Protein:** 15g • **Carbs:** 7g • **Fats:** 18g • **Fiber:** 2g

7. Pork Stuffed Peppers

4 Servings   **40 Minutes**

Cooking Tips:
* *Ensure the peppers are fully cooked but still retain their shape for the best texture. Pre-cook the stuffing to avoid undercooked pork.*

INGREDIENTS:

- 4 large bell peppers (about 480 g)
- 500 g ground pork
- 1 cup cauliflower rice (100 g)
- 1/2 cup cheddar cheese (56 g)
- 1/2 cup diced tomatoes (120 g)
- 1/4 cup chopped onions (30 g)
- 2 cloves garlic, minced (6 g)
- 1 tsp dried oregano (1 g)
- 1 tsp dried basil (1 g)
- 1 tbsp olive oil (15 ml)
- Salt and pepper to taste

INSTRUCTIONS:

1. Preheat oven to 375°F (190°C). Slice the tops off the bell peppers and remove seeds and membranes.

2. Heat olive oil in a skillet over medium heat. Add onions and garlic, cooking until softened.

3. Add ground pork to the skillet and cook until browned. Stir in cauliflower rice, diced tomatoes, oregano, basil, salt, and pepper.

4. Stuff each bell pepper with the pork mixture and place in a baking dish.

5. Top each stuffed pepper with shredded cheddar cheese.

6. Bake for 25-30 minutes until peppers are tender and cheese is melted.

Nutritional Information (per 100 grams): Calories: 180 kcal • Protein: 14g • Carbs: 7g • Fats: 11g • Fiber: 2g

8. Keto Pork Meatballs

6 Servings   **30 Minutes**

Cooking Tips:
* *For even cooking, make sure meatballs are uniformly sized. Optionally, serve with a low-carb marinara sauce.*

INSTRUCTIONS:

1. Preheat oven to 375°F (190°C). Line a baking sheet with parchment paper.

2. Mix ground pork, almond flour, Parmesan cheese, egg, garlic, oregano, basil, salt, and pepper in a large bowl.

3. Form mixture into 1.5-inch meatballs and place on the baking sheet.

4. Brush meatballs with olive oil.

5. Bake for 20-25 minutes until cooked through and browned

INGREDIENTS:

- 500 g ground pork
- 1/4 cup almond flour (28 g)
- 1/4 cup grated Parmesan cheese (25 g)
- 1 large egg (50 g)
- 2 cloves garlic, minced (6 g)
- 1/2 tsp dried oregano (1 g)
- 1/2 tsp dried basil (1 g)
- 1/2 tsp salt (2.5 g)
- 1/4 tsp black pepper (0.5 g)
- 1 tbsp olive oil (15 ml)

Nutritional Information (per 100 grams): Calories: 250 kcal • Protein: 20g • Carbs: 2g • Fats: 18g • Fiber: 1g

9. Creamy Mushroom Pork Chops

4 Servings   **30 Minutes**

Cooking Tips:
• For a richer flavor, consider adding a splash of white wine or extra garlic to the sauce. Ensure the pork chops are well-seared for a better texture.

INGREDIENTS:

- 4 pork chops (600 g)
- 1 cup sliced mushrooms (80 g)
- 1/2 cup heavy cream (120 ml)
- 1/4 cup chicken broth (60 ml)
- 2 tbsp olive oil (30 ml)
- 2 cloves garlic, minced (6 g)
- 1/2 tsp dried thyme (1 g)
- 1/2 tsp salt (2.5 g)
- 1/4 tsp black pepper (0.5 g)

INSTRUCTIONS:

1. Heat olive oil in a skillet over medium-high heat. Season pork chops with salt and pepper and sear for 3-4 minutes per side.

2. Remove the pork chops and set aside. In the same skillet, add the garlic and mushrooms, cooking until the mushrooms are browned.

3. Stir in heavy cream, chicken broth, and thyme. Bring to a simmer and cook until the sauce thickens.

4. Return pork chops to the skillet, simmering for 10 minutes or until the pork reaches an internal temperature of 145°F (63°C).

Nutritional Information (per 100 grams): **Calories:** 250 kcal • **Protein:** 22g • **Carbs:** 4g • **Fats:** 16g • **Fiber:** 1g

10. Keto Pork Tacos

4 Servings   **20 Minutes**

Cooking Tips:
• For extra flavor, top with avocado slices or a dollop of sour cream. Use large lettuce leaves for wrapping to hold more of the filling.

INGREDIENTS:

- 500 g ground pork
- 1 tbsp olive oil (15 ml)
- 1 tbsp chili powder (8 g)
- 1 tsp cumin (2 g)
- 1/2 tsp garlic powder (1 g)
- 1/2 tsp onion powder (1 g)
- 1/2 tsp salt (2.5 g)
- 1/4 tsp black pepper (0.5 g)
- 1 cup shredded lettuce (60 g)
- 1/2 cup diced tomatoes (120 g)
- 1/4 cup chopped cilantro (10 g)
- Lime wedges for serving

INSTRUCTIONS:

1. Heat olive oil in a skillet over medium heat. Add ground pork and cook until browned.

2. Stir in chili powder, cumin, garlic powder, onion powder, salt, and pepper. Cook for an additional 5 minutes.

3. Serve pork in lettuce wraps, topped with diced tomatoes, chopped cilantro, and a squeeze of lime juice.

Nutritional Information (per 100 grams): **Calories:** 220 kcal • **Protein:** 18g • **Carbs:** 5g • **Fats:** 15g • **Fiber:** 2g

11. Mustard-Crusted Pork Chops

🍴 4 Servings   🕐 30 Minutes

INGREDIENTS:

- 4 bone-in pork chops (600 g)
- 1/4 cup Dijon mustard (60 g)
- 1/2 cup almond flour (56 g)
- 1/4 cup grated Parmesan cheese (25 g)
- 1 tbsp dried rosemary (2 g)
- 1 tbsp dried thyme (2 g)
- 1/2 tsp salt (2.5 g)
- 1/4 tsp black pepper (0.5 g)
- 1 tbsp olive oil (15 ml)

INSTRUCTIONS:

1. Preheat oven to 400°F (200°C). Line a baking sheet with parchment paper.

2. Brush pork chops with Dijon mustard. Mix almond flour, Parmesan cheese, rosemary, thyme, salt, and pepper in a bowl.

3. Coat each pork chop with the almond flour mixture and place on the baking sheet.

4. Bake for 20-25 minutes or until the internal temperature reaches 145°F (63°C).

Nutritional Information (per 100 grams): **Calories:** 290 kcal • **Protein:** 25g • **Carbs:** 4g • **Fats:** 20g • **Fiber:** 1g

12. Keto Sweet and Sour Pork

🍴 4 Servings   🕐 30 Minutes

INGREDIENTS:

- 500 g pork tenderloin, cubed
- 1 cup diced bell peppers (120 g)
- 1 cup diced zucchini (120 g)
- 1/4 cup apple cider vinegar (60 ml)
- 2 tbsp erythritol (24 g)
- 2 tbsp soy sauce or coconut aminos (30 ml)
- 1 tbsp olive oil (15 ml)
- 2 cloves garlic, minced (6 g)
- 1 tsp ginger, minced (2 g)
- 1/4 tsp salt (1.25 g)
- 1/4 tsp black pepper (0.5 g)

INSTRUCTIONS:

1. Heat olive oil in a large skillet over medium-high heat. Add garlic and ginger, cooking for 1 minute.

2. Add cubed pork tenderloin and cook until browned.

3. Stir in bell peppers and zucchini, cooking for 5-7 minutes until vegetables are tender.

4. Mix apple cider vinegar, erythritol, soy sauce, salt, and pepper in a small bowl. Pour over pork and vegetables.

5. Simmer for an additional 5 minutes until sauce is thickened.

Nutritional Information (per 100 grams): **Calories:** 210 kcal • **Protein:** 20g • **Carbs:** 6g • **Fats:** 12g • **Fiber:** 2g

CHAPTER 7

Beef & Lamb Recipes

1. Keto Beef Stroganoff

🍴 4 Servings   🕐 30 Minutes

INGREDIENTS:

• 500 g beef sirloin or tenderloin, sliced into strips •1/2 cup beef broth (120 ml)
• 1 cup sliced mushrooms (80 g)
• 1/2 cup sour cream (120 g)
• 2 tbsp olive oil (30 ml)
• 1 medum onion, finely chopped (110 g)
• 2 cloves garlic, minced (6 g)
• 1 tbsp Worcestershire sauce (15 ml)
• 1 tsp paprika (2 g)
• Salt and pepper to taste

INSTRUCTIONS:

1. Heat olive oil in a large skillet over medium-high heat. Add onions and garlic, cooking until softened.

2. Add beef strips and cook until browned on all sides.

3. Stir in mushrooms, paprika, Worcestershire sauce, salt, and pepper. Cook for 5 minutes.

4. Pour in beef broth and simmer for 10 minutes until the sauce reduces slightly.

5. Reduce heat to low and stir in sour cream until well combined and heated.

Nutritional Information (per 100 grams): **Calories:** 220 kcal • **Protein:** 20g • **Carbs:** 5g • **Fats:** 15g • **Fiber:** 1g

2. Garlic Herb Crusted Lamb Chops

🍴 4 Servings   🕐 25 Minutes

INGREDIENTS:

• 8 lamb chops (600 g)
• 3 cloves garlic, minced (9 g)
• 2 tbsp fresh rosemary, chopped (3 g)
• 2 tbsp fresh thyme, chopped (3 g)
• 1/4 cup grated Parmesan cheese (25 g)
• 2 tbsp olive oil (30 ml)
• Salt and pepper to taste

INSTRUCTIONS:

1. Preheat oven to 400°F (200°C). Line a baking sheet with parchment paper.

2. Mix garlic, rosemary, thyme, Parmesan cheese, olive oil, salt, and pepper in a small bowl.

3. Rub the mixture onto both sides of the lamb chops.

4.Place lamb chops on the baking sheet and roast for 15-20 minutes, or until the internal temperature reaches 145°F (63°C) for medium-rare.

Nutritional Information (per 100 grams): **Calories:** 290 kcal • **Protein:** 25g • **Carbs:** 2g • **Fats:** 20g • **Fiber:** 0g

3. Keto Shepherd's Pie

🍴 4 Servings   🕐 45 Minutes

Cooking Tips:
• Ensure the cauliflower is well-drained before blending to avoid a watery mash. For a crispy top, broil the pie for a few minutes at the end of cooking.

INGREDIENTS:

• 500g ground beef •150g diced onions
• 1 cup diced mushrooms (80 g)
• 1/2 cup beef broth (120 ml)
• 2 tbsp tomato paste (30 g)
• 1 tsp dried thyme (1 g)
• 1/2 tsp salt • 1/4 tsp black pepper
  For the Cauliflower Mash:
• 1 large head cauliflower (about 800 g), chopped
• 60 ml heavy cream • 28 g butter
• Salt and pepper to taste

INSTRUCTIONS:

1. Preheat oven to 375°F (190°C).

2. For the Meat Filling: In a skillet, cook ground beef with onions until browned. Add mushrooms and cook until softened. Stir in beef broth, tomato paste, thyme, salt, and pepper. Simmer for 10 minutes.

3. For the Cauliflower Mash: Steam cauliflower until tender. Blend with heavy cream, butter, salt, and pepper until smooth.

4. Transfer the meat filling to a baking dish. Spread cauliflower mash evenly over the top.

5. Bake for 20-25 minutes until the mash is golden and the filling is bubbly.

Nutritional Information (per 100 grams): **Calories:** 220 kcal • **Protein:** 15g • **Carbs:** 6g • **Fats:** 15g • **Fiber:** 2g

4. Grilled Ribeye Steak

🍴 2 Servings   🕐 15 Minutes

Cooking Tips:
• For the best flavor, let the steaks come to room temperature before grilling. Use a meat thermometer to check for doneness.

INSTRUCTIONS:

1. Preheat the grill to high heat.

2. Rub steaks with olive oil, garlic, rosemary, thyme, salt, and pepper.

3. Grill steaks for 4-5 minutes per side for medium-rare, or adjust time for desired doneness.

4. Let steaks rest for 5 minutes before slicing.

INGREDIENTS:

• 2 ribeye steaks (each 300 g)
• 2 tbsp olive oil (30 ml)
• 2 cloves garlic, minced (6 g)
• 1 tsp dried rosemary (1 g)
• 1 tsp dried thyme (1 g)
• Salt and pepper to taste

Nutritional Information (per 100 grams): **Calories:** 250 kcal • **Protein:** 23g • **Carbs:** 0g • **Fats:** 17g • **Fiber:** 0g

5. Keto Meatloaf

🍴 4 Servings   🕐 1 Hour

Cooking Tips:
• Use a meat thermometer to ensure the meatloaf is fully cooked. For extra flavor, top with a bit of sugar-free ketchup before baking.

INSTRUCTIONS:

1. Preheat oven to 350°F (175°C). Line a loaf pan with parchment paper.

2. In a large bowl, combine all ingredients and mix well.

3. Transfer the mixture to the loaf pan and shape it into a loaf.

4. Bake for 45-50 minutes until the internal temperature reaches 160°F (71°C).

5. Let the meatloaf rest before slicing.

INGREDIENTS:

• 500 g ground beef
• 1/2 cup almond flour (56 g)
• 1/4 cup grated Parmesan cheese (25 g)
• 1 large egg (50 g)
• 1/2 cup chopped onions (60 g)
• 2 cloves garlic, minced (6 g)
• 1/4 cup sugar-free ketchup (60 g)
• 1 tsp dried oregano (1 g)
• 1/2 tsp salt (2.5 g)
• 1/4 tsp black pepper (0.5 g)

Nutritional Information (per 100 grams): **Calories:** 270 kcal • **Protein:** 20g • **Carbs:** 5g • **Fats:** 20g • **Fiber:** 2g

6. Moroccan Spiced Lamb

🍴 4 Servings   🕐 40 Minutes

Cooking Tips:
• Adjust the spice blend to your taste preference. For a thicker sauce, simmer longer or add a thickening agent like xanthan gum.

INSTRUCTIONS:

1. Heat olive oil in a large skillet over medium heat. Add onions and garlic, cooking until softened.

2. Add lamb and brown on all sides.

3. Stir in the Moroccan spice blend, tomatoes, and beef broth. Simmer for 25 minutes until the lamb is tender.

4. Garnish with chopped cilantro before serving.

INGREDIENTS:

• 600 g lamb shoulder, cubed
• 2 tbsp olive oil (30 ml)
• 2 tbsp Moroccan spice blend (16 g)
• 1 cup diced tomatoes (240 g)
• 1/2 cup diced onions (60 g)
• 2 cloves garlic, minced (6 g)
• 1 cup beef broth (240 ml)
• 1/4 cup chopped cilantro (10 g)
• Salt and pepper to taste

Nutritional Information (per 100 grams): **Calories:** 290 kcal • **Protein:** 24g • **Carbs:** 7g • **Fats:** 18g • **Fiber:** 2g

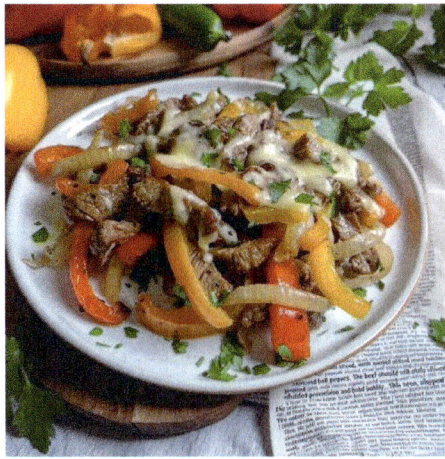

7. Keto Philly Cheesesteak

4 Servings   **30 Minutes**

INGREDIENTS:

- 500 g thinly sliced beef sirloin
- 1 tbsp olive oil (15 ml)
- 1 cup sliced bell peppers (120 g)
- 1 cup sliced onions (150 g)
- 1 cup shredded provolone cheese (120 g)
- 2 cloves garlic, minced (6 g)
- Salt and pepper to taste

INSTRUCTIONS:

1. Heat olive oil in a large skillet over medium-high heat. Add onions and bell peppers, cooking until softened.

2. Add garlic and beef slices until beef is browned and cooked through.

3. Season with salt and pepper.

4. Top with shredded provolone cheese and cook until melted.

Nutritional Information (per 100 grams): Calories: 290 kcal • **Protein:** 23g • **Carbs:** 6g • **Fats:** 20g • **Fiber:** 2g

8. Keto Burger with Cheese and Bacon

4 Servings   **20 Minutes**

INGREDIENTS:

- 500 g ground beef (80/20 fat ratio)
- 4 slices cheddar cheese (80 g)
- 8 strips bacon (200 g)
- 1 large egg (50 g)
- 1/4 cup almond flour (28 g)
- 1 tsp garlic powder (2 g)
- 1/2 tsp onion powder (1 g)
- Salt and pepper to taste
- Lettuce leaves for wrapping

INSTRUCTIONS:

1. Preheat the grill or skillet over medium-high heat.

2. Mix ground beef with egg, almond flour, garlic powder, onion powder, salt, and pepper in a bowl. Form into four patties.

3. Cook bacon in a skillet until crispy. Drain on paper towels.

4. Grill or pan-fry the beef patties for 4-5 minutes per side or until they reach your desired doneness.

5. Place a slice of cheddar cheese on each patty during the last minute of cooking to melt.6. Assemble burgers by wrapping patties with bacon and cheese in lettuce leaves.

Nutritional Information (per 100 grams): Calories: 280 kcal • **Protein:** 22g • **Carbs:** 2g • **Fats:** 20g • **Fiber:** 1g

11. Lamb Kofta Kebabs

4 Servings　　**30 Minutes**

INSTRUCTIONS:

1. Preheat the grill or oven broiler to high heat.

2. Mix ground lamb with parsley, mint, onion, garlic, cumin, coriander, paprika, salt, and pepper. Shape the mixture into kebabs and skewer.

3. Grill or broil kebabs for 10-12 minutes, turning occasionally until cooked through.

INGREDIENTS:

• 500 g ground lamb
• 1/4 cup chopped fresh parsley -15 g
• 1/4 cup chopped fresh mint (15 g)
• 1 small onion, grated (70 g)
• 2 cloves garlic, minced (6 g)
• 1 tsp ground cumin (2 g)
• 1 tsp ground coriander (2 g)
• 1/2 tsp paprika (1 g)
• 1/2 tsp salt (2.5 g)
• 1/4 tsp black pepper (0.5 g)

Nutritional Information (per 100 grams): **Calories:** 250 kcal • **Protein:** 20g • **Carbs:** 3g • **Fats:** 17g • **Fiber:** 1g

12. Keto Beef Bourguignon

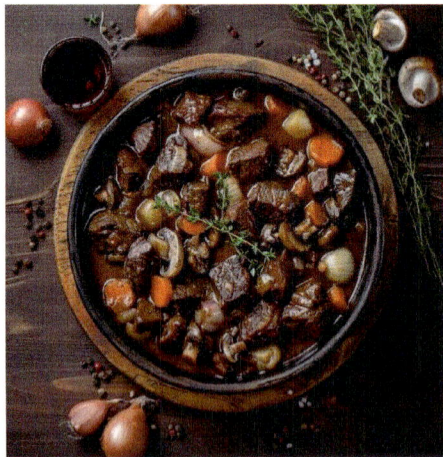

6 Servings　　**2 Hours**

INSTRUCTIONS:

1. Heat olive oil in a large pot over medium heat. Brown the beef cubes in batches, then set aside.

2. In the same pot, add onions and garlic and cook until softened.

3. Return beef to the pot and stir in wine (if using), beef broth, tomato paste, thyme, and bay leaf. Bring to a simmer.

4. Add mushrooms, carrots, and pearl onions. Simmer covered for 1.5 hours or until beef is tender.

5. Season with salt and pepper to taste.

INGREDIENTS:

• 500 g beef chuck, cut into cubes
• 1 tbsp olive oil (15 ml)
• 1 cup diced onions (150 g)
• 2 cloves garlic, minced (6 g)
• Red wine 240 ml
• 2 cups beef broth (480 ml)
• 1 tbsp tomato paste (15 g)
• 1 tsp dried thyme •1 bay leaf
• 1 cup sliced mushrooms (70 g)
• 1/2 cup chopped carrots (60 g)
• 1/2 cup pearl onions (70 g)
• Salt and pepper to taste

Nutritional Information (per 100 grams): **Calories:** 220 kcal • **Protein:** 20g • **Carbs:** 6g • **Fats:** 13g • **Fiber:** 2g

CHAPTER 8
Fish & Seafood Recipes

1. Lemon Garlic Butter Shrimp

4 Servings   **15 Minutes**

Cooking Tips:
• *Do not overcook shrimp, as they can become tough. Adjust the lemon juice to taste if you prefer more or less acidity*

INGREDIENTS:

• 500 g large shrimp, peeled and deveined
• 3 tbsp unsalted butter (42 g)
• 3 cloves garlic, minced (9 g)
• Juice of 1 lemon (30 ml)
• 1 tsp lemon zest (2 g)
• 2 tbsp fresh parsley, chopped (8 g)
• Salt and pepper to taste

INSTRUCTIONS:

1. Heat butter in a large skillet over medium heat.

2. Add minced garlic and cook until fragrant (about 1 minute).

3. Add shrimp, salt, and pepper. Cook until shrimp are pink and opaque (about 2-3 minutes per side).

4. Stir in lemon juice, lemon zest, and parsley.

5. Serve immediately.

Nutritional Information (per 100 grams): **Calories:** 210 kcal • **Protein:** 25g • **Carbs:** 2g • **Fats:** 12g • **Fiber:** 0g

2. Coconut Shrimp

2 Servings   **25 Minutes**

Cooking Tips:
• *Ensure shrimp are well-coated for a crispy texture. If baking, flip halfway through for even browning.*

INGREDIENTS:

• 500 g large shrimp, peeled and deveined
• 1 cup unsweetened shredded coconut (80 g)
• 1/2 cup almond flour (56 g)
• 2 large eggs (100 g)
• 1/2 tsp paprika (1 g)
• 1/2 tsp garlic powder (1 g)
• Salt and pepper to taste
• Coconut oil, for frying (as needed)

INSTRUCTIONS:

1. Preheat oven to 400°F (200°C) if baking.

2. Mix shredded coconut, almond flour, paprika, garlic powder, salt, and pepper in a bowl.

3. Beat eggs in another bowl.

4. Dip each shrimp in eggs, then coat with the coconut mixture.

5. Fry in coconut oil over medium heat until golden brown and cook through (about 2-3 minutes per side), or bake on a baking sheet for 15-20 minutes.

Nutritional Information (per 100 grams): **Calories:** 290 kcal • **Protein:** 22g • **Carbs:** 10g • **Fats:** 18g • **Fiber:** 4g

3. Keto Fish Tacos

🍴 **4 Servings** 🕐 **25 Minutes**

Cooking Tips:
• *Use sturdy lettuce leaves like Romaine for the taco shells. Adjust seasoning based on personal preference and avoid overcooking the fish to keep it tender.*

INSTRUCTIONS:

1. Preheat oven to 400°F (200°C).

2. Mix paprika, cumin, garlic powder, salt, and pepper. Rub the seasoning onto the fish fillets.

3. Place fish fillets on a baking sheet and drizzle with olive oil.

4. Bake for 15-20 minutes or until fish flakes easily with a fork..

5. Break the fish into pieces and serve in lettuce leaves with shredded cabbage, avocado slices, sour cream, and a squeeze of lime juice.

INGREDIENTS:

• 500 g white fish fillets (such as cod or tilapia)
• 1 tbsp olive oil (15 ml)
• 1 tsp paprika (2 g)
• 1/2 tsp cumin (1 g)
• 1/2 tsp garlic powder (1 g)
• Salt and pepper to taste
• 4 large lettuce leaves
• 1 cup shredded cabbage (70 g)
• 1/2 avocado, sliced (75 g)
• 2 tbsp sour cream (30 g)
• 1 tbsp lime juice (15 ml)

Nutritional Information (per 100 grams): Calories: 180 kcal • **Protein:** 22g • **Carbs:** 5g • **Fats:** 8g • **Fiber:** 2g

4. Garlic Butter Scallops

🍴 **4 Servings** 🕐 **15 Minutes**

Cooking Tips:
• *Do not overcrowd the skillet; cook scallops in batches if necessary. Ensure the skillet is hot enough before adding scallops to achieve a nice sear*

INSTRUCTIONS:

1. Pat scallops dry with paper towels and season with salt and pepper.

2. Heat butter in a large skillet over medium-high heat.

3. Add garlic and cook for 1 minute until fragrant.

4. Add scallops to the skillet and cook for 2-3 minutes per side, until golden brown and cooked through.

5. Stir in lemon juice and parsley before serving.

INGREDIENTS:

• 500 g sea scallops
• 3 tbsp unsalted butter (42 g)
• 3 cloves garlic, minced (9 g)
• 1 tbsp fresh parsley, chopped (4 g)
• 1 tbsp lemon juice (15 ml)
• Salt and pepper to taste

Nutritional Information (per 100 grams): Calories: 155 kcal • **Protein:** 22g • **Carbs:** 1g • **Fats:** 7g • **Fiber:** 0g

5. Keto Crab Cakes

🍴 **4 Servings**   🕐 **20 Minutes**

Cooking Tips:
• Ensure the crab meat is well-drained to avoid excess moisture. Chill the patties before cooking to help them hold together better

INGREDIENTS:

- 400 g crab meat (fresh or canned)
- 1 large egg (50 g)
- 1/4 cup almond flour (28 g)
- 2 tbsp mayonnaise (30 g)
- 1 tbsp Dijon mustard (15 g)
- 1/2 tsp paprika (1 g)
- 1/2 tsp garlic powder (1 g)
- Salt and pepper to taste
- 2 tbsp olive oil (30 ml, for frying)

INSTRUCTIONS:

1. In a bowl, combine crab meat, egg, almond flour, mayonnaise, mustard, paprika, garlic powder, salt, and pepper.

2. Form the mixture into 8 patties.

3. Heat olive oil in a skillet over medium heat.

4. Cook crab cakes for 3-4 minutes per side, until golden brown and crispy.

5. Serve hot.

Nutritional Information (per 100 grams): **Calories:** 220 kcal • **Protein:** 20g • **Carbs:** 3g • **Fats:** 14g • **Fiber:** 1g

6. Keto Salmon Patties

🍴 **4 Servings**   🕐 **20 Minutes**

Cooking Tips:
• Use a non-stick skillet or well-seasoned cast iron to avoid sticking. Refrigerate the patties for about 30 minutes before frying to help them hold together

INSTRUCTIONS:

1. Mix salmon, egg, almond flour, mayonnaise, dill, garlic powder, salt, and pepper in a bowl.

2. Form the mixture into eight patties.

3. Heat olive oil in a skillet over medium heat.

4. Fry patties for 3-4 minutes per side until golden brown.

5. Serve warm.

INGREDIENTS:

- 400 g canned salmon, drained and flaked
- 1 large egg (50 g)
- 1/4 cup almond flour (28 g)
- 2 tbsp mayonnaise (30 g)
- 1 tbsp fresh dill, chopped (4 g)
- 1/2 tsp garlic powder (1 g)
- Salt and pepper to taste
- 2 tbsp olive oil (30 ml, for frying)

Nutritional Information (per 100 grams): **Calories:** 240 kcal • **Protein:** 22g • **Carbs:** 3g • **Fats:** 15g • **Fiber:** 1g

7. Seared Ahi Tuna

🍴 4 Servings   🕐 15 Minutes

Cooking Tips:
• *Make sure the skillet is very hot before adding the tuna to get a good sear. Avoid overcooking to keep the tuna tender and flavorful.*

INSTRUCTIONS:

1. Season tuna steaks with salt, pepper, and sesame seeds.

2. Heat olive oil in a skillet over high heat.

3. Sear tuna for 1-2 minutes per side, until the outside is browned but the center is rare.

4. In a small bowl, mix soy sauce, ginger, and garlic.

5. Serve tuna with soy sauce mixture.

INGREDIENTS:

• 4 ahi tuna steaks (150 g each, 600 g total)
• 2 tbsp olive oil (30 ml)
• 1 tbsp sesame seeds (8 g)
• 1 tbp soy sauce (15 ml)
• 1 tsp grated ginger (2 g)
• 1 clove garlic, minced (3 g)
• Salt and pepper to taste

Nutritional Information (per 100 grams): Calories: 150 kcal • Protein: 25g • Carbs: 1g • Fats: 5g • Fiber: 0g

8. Keto Clam Chowder

🍴 4 Servings   🕐 30 Minutes

Cooking Tips:
• *For a thicker chowder, blend part of the cauliflower before adding the clams. Adjust seasoning according to your taste.*

INSTRUCTIONS:

1. In a large pot, cook bacon over medium heat until crispy. Remove and set aside.

2. In the same pot, sauté celery, onion, and garlic in bacon fat until soft.

3. Add cauliflower and cook for another 5 minutes.

4. Pour in chicken broth and add thyme and bay leaf. Simmer for 10 minutes until cauliflower is tender.

5. Stir in heavy cream and clams. Heat through, but do not boil.

6. Season with salt and pepper and garnish with crispy bacon and parsley before serving.

INGREDIENTS:

• 2 cans (400 g each) clams, drained (total 800 g)
• 4 slices bacon, chopped (100 g)
• 1 cup celery, diced (120 g)
• 1/2 cup onion, diced (75 g)
• 2 cloves garlic, minced (6 g)
• 1 cup cauliflower florets (100 g)
• 2 cups chicken broth (480 ml)
• 1 cup heavy cream (240 ml)
• 1 tsp dried thyme (1 g)
• 1 bay leaf •Salt and pepper to taste
• 2 tbsp fresh parsley, chopped (8 g)

Nutritional Information (per 100 grams): Calories: 190 kcal • Protein: 10g • Carbs: 5g • Fats: 14g • Fiber: 1g

9. Blackened Salmon

4 Servings

15 Minutes

Cooking Tips:
• Make sure the skillet is very hot before searing to get a crispy crust. Use a fish spatula for easy flipping

INSTRUCTIONS:

1. Preheat oven to 400°F (200°C).

2. Mix paprika, garlic powder, onion powder, cayenne pepper, thyme, oregano, salt, and pepper.

3. Rub the spice mixture evenly over the salmon fillets.

4. Heat olive oil in a skillet over medium-high heat.

5. Sear salmon fillets for 2 minutes per side, then transfer to a baking sheet.

6. Bake for 6-8 minutes, until salmon flakes easily with a fork.

7. Serve with lemon wedges.

INGREDIENTS:

• 4 salmon fillets (150 g each, 600 g total)
• 2 tbsp olive oil (30 ml)
• 1 tbsp smoked paprika (6 g)
• 1 tsp garlic powder (3 g)
• 1 tp onion powder (3 g)
• 1/2 tsp cayenne pepper (1 g)
• 1/2 tsp dried thyme (1 g)
• 1/2 tsp dried oregano (1 g)
• Salt and pepper to taste
• Lemon wedges for serving

Nutritional Information (per 100 grams): Calories: 200 kcal • **Protein:** 24g • **Carbs:** 0g • **Fats:** 12g • **Fiber:** 0g

10. Crab Stuffed Mushrooms

4 Servings

25 Minutes

Cooking Tips:
• Ensure mushrooms are thoroughly cleaned before stuffing. Use fresh crab meat for the best flavor.

INSTRUCTIONS:

1. Preheat oven to 375°F (190°C).

2. Mix crab meat, cream cheese, mayonnaise, Parmesan cheese, parsley, garlic, lemon juice, salt, and pepper in a bowl.

3. Spoon the mixture into mushroom caps.

4. Place stuffed mushrooms on a baking sheet.

5. Bake for 15-20 minutes, until mushrooms are tender and tops are golden.

6. Serve warm.

INGREDIENTS:

• 12 large mushrooms, stems removed (300 g)
• 200 g crab meat, lump or imitation
• 60 g cream cheese, softened
• 1/4 cup mayonnaise (60 g)
• 1/4 cup grated Parmesan cheese (25 g)
• 1 tbsp fresh parsley, chopped (4 g)
• 1 clove garlic, minced (3 g)
• 1/2 tsp lemon juice (2 ml)
• Salt and pepper to taste

Nutritional Information (per 100 grams): Calories: 160 kcal • **Protein:** 12g • **Carbs:** 4g • **Fats:** 11g • **Fiber:** 1g

CHAPTER 9

Vegan, Vegetables & Vegetarian Recipes

1. Keto Cauliflower Mac and Cheese

4 Servings

30 Minutes

Cooking Tips:
• Ensure the cauliflower is well-drained to avoid a watery cheese sauce. You can also sprinkle extra cheese on top before baking for a more indulgent finish

INGREDIENTS:

- 500 g cauliflower florets
- 1 cup heavy cream (240 ml)
- 1 cup shredded sharp cheddar cheese (112 g)
- 1/2 cup grated Parmesan cheese (50 g)
- 2 tbsp butter (28 g)
- 1/2 tsp garlic powder (1 g)
- 1/2 tsp paprika (1 g)
- Salt and pepper to taste

INSTRUCTIONS:

1. Preheat oven to 375°F (190°C).

2. Steam cauliflower florets until tender, about 10 minutes.

3. In a saucepan, melt butter over medium heat. Add heavy cream and bring to a simmer.

4. Stir in cheddar and Parmesan cheese until melted and smooth.

5. Season with garlic powder, paprika, salt, and pepper.

6. Combine cauliflower with cheese sauce and transfer to a baking dish.

7. Bake for 15-20 minutes until bubbly and golden on top.

Nutritional Information (per 100 grams): **Calories:** 190 kcal • **Protein:** 8g • **Carbs:** 6g • **Fats:** 16g • **Fiber:** 3g

2. Bacon-Wrapper Asparagus

4 Servings

30 Minutes

Cooking Tips:
• For extra flavor, try adding a sprinkle of grated Parmesan cheese during the last few minutes of cooking.

INGREDIENTS:

- 400 grams fresh asparagus spears
- 200 grams bacon strips (about 8 slices)
- 10 grams olive oil
- 2 grams garlic powder (optional)
- Salt and pepper to taste

INSTRUCTIONS:

1. Wash and trim the woody ends of the asparagus spears.

Wrap with Bacon:

2. Wrap each asparagus spear with a strip of bacon. Secure with a toothpick if needed.

3. Drizzle the wrapped asparagus with olive oil and sprinkle with garlic powder, salt, and pepper.

4. Heat a gas grill to medium heat. Place the bacon-wrapped asparagus on the grill.

5. Cook for 10-15 minutes, turning occasionally, until the bacon is crispy and the asparagus is tender.

6. Remove from the grill and serve hot.

Nutritional Information (per 100 grams): **Calories:** 220 kcal • **Protein:** 12g • **Carbs:** 3g • **Fats:** 18g • **Fiber:** 1g

3. Keto Zucchini Fries

4 Servings   **25 Minutes**

Cooking Tips:
• Ensure the zucchini fries are spaced out on the baking sheet to avoid steaming. For extra crispiness, flip the fries halfway through baking.

INSTRUCTIONS:

1. Preheat oven to 425°F (220°C).

2. Mix almond flour, Parmesan cheese, paprika, garlic powder, onion powder, salt, and pepper in a bowl.

3. Dip zucchini fries into beaten eggs, then coat them with almond flour.

4. Arrange a single layer of coated zucchini fries on a baking sheet.

5. Drizzle with olive oil and bake for 20-25 minutes until golden and crispy

INGREDIENTS:

• 2 medium zucchinis, cut into fries (300 g)
• 1/2 cup almond flour (50 g)
• 1/2 cup grated Parmesan cheese (50 g)
• 1 tsp paprika (2 g)
• 1/2 tsp garlic powder (1 g)
• 1/2 tsp onion powder (1 g)
• 2 lage eggs, beaten (100 g)
• Salt and pepper to taste
• 1 tbsp olive oil (15 ml)

Nutritional Information (per 100 grams): Calories: 160 kcal • **Protein:** 7g • **Carbs:** 8g • **Fats:** 11g • **Fiber:** 3g

4. Keto Mashed Cauliflower

4 Servings   **20 Minutes**

Cooking Tips:
• Ensure cauliflower is well-drained before mashing to avoid a watery texture. For extra creaminess, you can add more butter or cream.

INSTRUCTIONS:

1. Steam cauliflower florets until very tender, about 10 minutes.

2. Drain well and place in a food processor.

3. Add heavy cream, butter, cheddar cheese, garlic, salt, and pepper.

4. Process until smooth and creamy.

5. Adjust seasoning as needed and serve warm.

INGREDIENTS:

• 600 g cauliflower florets
• 1/4 cup heavy cream (60 ml)
• 2 tbsp butter (28 g)
• 1/2 cup shredded cheddar cheese (56 g)
• 2 cloves garlic, minced (6 g)
• Salt and pepper to taste

Nutritional Information (per 100 grams): Calories: 130 kcal • **Protein:** 5g • **Carbs:** 5g • **Fats:** 11g • **Fiber:** 2g

5. Cheesy Baked Zucchini

🍴 **4 Servings**   🕐 **25 Minutes**

Cooking Tips:
• For a crispier texture, you can broil the zucchini for the last 2 minutes of baking.

INSTRUCTIONS:

1. Preheat oven to 375°F (190°C).

2. Toss zucchini slices with olive oil, oregano, garlic powder, salt, and pepper.

3. Arrange zucchini in a single layer on a baking sheet.

4. Bake for 15 minutes, then sprinkle with mozzarella and Parmesan cheese.

5. Return to oven and bake for 10 minutes until cheese is melted and bubbly.

INGREDIENTS:

• 4 medium zucchinis, sliced (400 g)
• 1 cup shredded mozzarella cheese (112 g)
•1/4 cup grated Parmesan cheese (25 g)
• 1/2 tsp dried oregano (1 g)
• 1/2 tsp garlic powder (1 g)
• 1 tbsp olive oil (15 ml)
• Salt and pepper to taste

Nutritional Information (per 100 grams): **Calories:** 130 kcal • **Protein:** 7g • **Carbs:** 6g • **Fats:** 9g • **Fiber:** 2g

6. Cauliflower Rice Pilaf

🍴 **4 Servings**   🕐 **20 Minutes**

Cooking Tips:
• For extra flavor, consider adding a splash of lemon juice or a pinch of paprika.

INSTRUCTIONS:

1. Heat olive oil in a large skillet over medium heat.

2. Add onion and bell peppers; cook until softened, about 5 minutes.

3. Stir in garlic and thyme; cook for one more minute.

4. Add riced cauliflower and cook, stirring occasionally, for about 10 minutes until tender and slightly golden.

5. Season with salt, pepper, and parsley before serving.

INGREDIENTS:

• 1 medium cauliflower head (600 g), riced
• 2 tbsp olive oil (30 ml)
• 1/2 cup diced onion (75 g)
• 1/2 cup diced bell peppers (75 g)
• 1/4 cup chopped parsley (15 g)
• 2 cloves garlic, minced (6 g)
• 1/2 tsp dried thyme (1 g)
• Salt and pepper to taste

Nutritional Information (per 100 grams): **Calories:** 80 kcal • **Protein:** 3g • **Carbs:** 3g • **Fats:** 6g • **Fiber:** 3g

7. Keto Ratatouille

🍴 **4 Servings** 🕐 **45 Minutes**

Cooking Tips:
• *For a richer flavor, try adding a splash of balsamic vinegar or a sprinkle of Parmesan cheese before serving*

INGREDIENTS:

• 1 medium eggplant, diced (300 g)
• 1 zucchini, diced (200 g)
• 1 bell pepper, diced (150 g)
• 1 cup diced tomatoes (240 g)
• 1/4 cup olive oil (60 ml)
• 2 cloves garlic, minced (6 g)
• 1 tsp dried basil (1 g)
• 1 tsp dried oregano (1 g)
• Salt and pepper to taste

INSTRUCTIONS:

1. Preheat oven to 400°F (200°C).

2. In a large bowl, toss eggplant, zucchini, bell pepper with olive oil, garlic, basil, oregano, salt, and pepper.

3. Spread vegetables on a baking sheet in a single layer.

4. Roast for 25-30 minutes, stirring halfway through, until tender and slightly caramelized.

5. Stir in diced tomatoes and cook for an additional 5 minutes

Nutritional Information (per 100 grams): **Calories:** 100 kcal • **Protein:** 2g • **Carbs:** 9g • **Fats:** 8g • **Fiber:** 4g

8. Spinach Artichoke Dip

🍴 **6 Servings** 🕐 **30 Minutes**

Cooking Tips:
• *Serve with keto-friendly vegetables or use as a topping for grilled chicken or fish. For added flavor, try incorporating a pinch of nutmeg or red pepper flakes*

INSTRUCTIONS:

1. Preheat oven to 375°F (190°C).

2. In a bowl, combine cream cheese, sour cream, Parmesan cheese, mozzarella cheese, garlic, salt, and pepper.

3. Fold in spinach and artichokes.

4. Transfer the mixture to a baking dish.

5. Bake for 20-25 minutes until bubbly and golden on top.

INGREDIENTS:

• 1 cup frozen spinach, thawed and drained (150 g)
• 1 cup canned artichoke hearts, chopped (120 g)
• 1 cup cream cheese, softened (240 g)
• 120 g sour cream
• 50 g shredded Parmesan cheese
• 55 g shredded mozzarella cheese
• 2 cloves garlic, minced (6 g)
• Salt and pepper to taste

Nutritional Information (per 100 grams): **Calories:** 250 kcal • **Protein:** 10g • **Carbs:** 6g • **Fats:** 21g • **Fiber:** 2g

9. Keto Avocado Pesto Zoodles

4 Servings   **15 Minutes**

Cooking Tips:
• To keep the zoodles fresh, toss them with pesto just before serving.

INGREDIENTS:

• 4 medium zucchinis (600 g), spiralized into noodles
• 2 ripe avocados (300 g)
• 1/2 cup fresh basil leaves (15 g)
• 1/4 cup pine nuts (30 g)
• 25 g grated Parmesan cheese
• 2 cloves garlic (6 g)
• 1/4 cup olive oil (60 ml)
• Juice of 1 lemon (30 ml)
• Salt and pepper to taste•

INSTRUCTIONS:

1. Combine avocados, basil, pine nuts, Parmesan cheese, garlic, olive oil, lemon juice, salt, and pepper in a food processor. Blend until smooth.

2. Toss the spiralized zucchini noodles with the avocado pesto until well coated.

3. Serve immediately or chill before serving.

Nutritional Information (per 100 grams): **Calories:** 220 kcal • **Protein:** 5g • **Carbs:**8 g • **Fats:** 20g • **Fiber:** 6g

10. Spicy Cauliflower Bites

4 Servings   **30 Minutes**

Cooking Tips:
• For extra crispiness, you can broil the cauliflower for the last 5 minutes of baking.

INGREDIENTS:

• 1 medium cauliflower head (600 g), cut into florets
• 1/4 cup olive oil (60 ml)
• 1/2 cup almond flour (48 g)
• 1/4 cup grated Parmesan cheese (25 g)
• 1 tsp smoked paprika (2 g)
• 1/2 tsp cayenne pepper (1 g)
• 1/2 tsp garlic powder (1 g)
• Salt to taste

INSTRUCTIONS:

1. Preheat oven to 400°F (200°C) and line a baking sheet with parchment paper.

2. In a large bowl, toss cauliflower florets with olive oil.

3. Mix almond flour, Parmesan cheese, paprika, cayenne pepper, garlic powder, and salt in another bowl.

4. Coat cauliflower florets with the almond flour mixture.

5. Spread florets on the baking sheet and bake for 25-30 minutes or until golden and crispy.

Nutritional Information (per 100 grams): **Calories:** 190 kcal • **Protein:** 5g • **Carbs:** 10g • **Fats:** 14g • **Fiber:** 5g

11. Vegan Keto Curry

🍴 **4 Servings**

🕐 **30 Minutes**

INGREDIENTS:

- 1 tbsp coconut oil (15 ml)
- 1 medium onion, diced (150 g)
- 3 cloves garlic, minced (9 g)
- 1 tbsp fresh ginger, minced (10 g)
- 1 medium cauliflower, cut into florets (600 g)
- 1 cup coconut milk (240 ml)
- 2 tbsp curry powder (12 g)
- 1 tsp turmeric •1 tsp cumin
- 1 cup chopped tomatoes (240 g)
- Salt and pepper to taste
- 1 cup fresh spinach (30 g)

INSTRUCTIONS:

1. Heat coconut oil in a large pan over medium heat. Sauté onion, garlic, and ginger until translucent.

2. Add curry powder, turmeric, and cumin; cook for another minute.

3. Stir in cauliflower and chopped tomatoes. Cook for 5 minutes.

4. Add coconut milk, simmer, and cook until cauliflower is tender, about 15 minutes.

5. Stir in fresh spinach until wilted. Season with salt and pepper.

Nutritional Information (per 100 grams): **Calories:** 100 kcal • **Protein:** 2g • **Carbs:** 8g • **Fats:** 8g • **Fiber:** 4g

12. Cauliflower Pizza Crust

🍴 **8 Servings**

🕐 **40 Minutes**
1 Large pizza

INSTRUCTIONS:

1. Preheat oven to 425°F (220°C). Line a baking sheet with parchment paper.

2. Microwave grated cauliflower for 5 minutes. Let cool, then squeeze out excess moisture using a clean kitchen towel.

3. Mix cauliflower, mozzarella, Parmesan, egg, oregano, garlic powder, salt, and pepper until well combined.

4. Spread the mixture onto the prepared baking sheet into a 12-inch round, pressing down firmly.

5. Bake for 20 minutes or until golden brown and crispy. Top with your favorite keto-friendly toppings and bake for an additional 10 minutes.

INGREDIENTS:

- 1 medium cauliflower, grated (500 g)
- 1 cup shredded mozzarella cheese (112 g)
- 1/4 cup grated Parmesan cheese (25 g)
- 1 large egg, beaten (50 g)
- 1 tsp dried oregano (1 g)
- 1/2 tsp garlic powder (1 g)
- Salt and pepper to taste

Nutritional Information (per 100 grams): **Calories:** 80 kcal • **Protein:** 6g • **Carbs:** 6g • **Fats:** 5g • **Fiber:** 3g

13. Keto Tofu Stir Fry

4 Servings　　**20 Minutes**

Cooking Tips:
• Press tofu to remove excess moisture for better texture and flavour.

INGREDIENTS:

- 1 block firm tofu, cubed (250 g)
- 2 tbsp coconut oil (30 ml)
- 1 bell pepper, sliced (150 g)
- 1 cup snap peas (100 g)
- 1 medium carrot, sliced (60 g)
- 2 tbsp soy sauce or tamari (30 ml)
- 1 tbsp sesame oil (15 ml)
- 1 tbsp fresh ginger, minced (10 g)
- 2 cloves garlic, minced (6 g)
- 1 tbsp sesame seeds (9 g)
- Salt and pepper to taste

INSTRUCTIONS:

1. Heat coconut oil in a large pan over medium-high heat. Add tofu and cook until golden brown on all sides, about 5-7 minutes.

2. Remove tofu and set aside. In the same pan, add bell pepper, snap peas, and carrot. Stir-fry for 5 minutes.

3. Add garlic, ginger, soy sauce, and sesame oil. Cook for another 2 minutes.

4. Return tofu to the pan, toss to combine, and cook for another minute.

5. Garnish with sesame seeds and serve.

Nutritional Information (per 100 grams): **Calories:** 120 kcal • **Protein:** 8g • **Carbs:** 7g • **Fats:** 8g • **Fiber:** 3g

14. Eggplant Lasagna

6 Servings　　**1 Hour**

Cooking Tips:
• Use a mandoline for even eggplant slices to ensure uniform cooking.

INGREDIENTS:

- 2 large eggplants, sliced (600 g)
- 2 tbsp olive oil (30 ml)
- 1 cup ricotta cheese (240 g)
- 110 g shredded mozzarella cheese
- 1 cup marinara sauce (240 g)
- 50 g grated Parmesan cheese
- 1 egg, beaten (50 g)
- 1 tsp dried basil (1 g)
- 1 tsp dried oregano (1 g)
- Salt and pepper to taste

INSTRUCTIONS:

1. Preheat oven to 375°F (190°C).

2. Brush eggplant slices with olive oil and roast on a baking sheet for 20 minutes, flipping halfway.

3. Mix ricotta cheese, egg, basil, oregano, salt, and pepper in a bowl.

4. Layer eggplant slices, ricotta mixture, marinara sauce, and mozzarella cheese in a baking dish. Repeat layers.

5. Top with Parmesan cheese and bake for 25-30 minutes, until bubbly and golden.

Nutritional Information (per 100 grams): **Calories:** 130 kcal • **Protein:** 7g • **Carbs:** 10g • **Fats:** 8g • **Fiber:** 4g

CHAPTER 10

Asian Stile Recipes

1. Keto Miso Soup

🍴 **4 Servings**   🕐 **15 Minutes**

Cooking Tips:
• Use low-sodium soy sauce or tamari to keep sodium levels in check. Be careful not to boil the soup once miso is added, as high heat can alter its flavor.

INSTRUCTIONS:

1. Heat the broth in a pot over medium heat.
2. Add the miso paste and stir until dissolved.
3. Add the mushrooms, green onions, and tofu. Simmer for 5 minutes.
4. Stir in soy sauce, ginger, and garlic powder.
5. Serve hot.

INGREDIENTS:

• 4 cups (960 ml) chicken or vegetable broth
• 3 tbsp (45 g) white miso paste
• 1/2 cup (50 g) sliced mushrooms
• 1/4 cup (30 g) chopped green onions
• 1/2 cup (60 g) tofu, cubed
• 1 tbsp (15 ml) soy sauce or tamari
• 1 tsp (1 g) grated ginger
• 1 tsp (1 g) garlic powder

Nutritional Information (per 100 grams): **Calories:** 25 kcal • **Protein:** 2g • **Carbs:** 3g • **Fats:** 1g • **Fiber:** 0,5g

2. Shrimp Pad Thai

🍴 **2 Servings**   🕐 **25 Minutes**

Cooking Tips:
• Use pre-shredded cabbage to save time and ensure even cooking.

INSTRUCTIONS:

1. Heat olive oil in a skillet over medium-high heat. Add garlic and cook for 1 minute.

2. Add shrimp and cook until pink and opaque, about 3-4 minutes. Remove shrimp and set aside.

3. Add shredded cabbage and stir-fry for 5 minutes in the same skillet.

4. Push cabbage to one side of the skillet, pour beaten eggs into the empty side, and scramble until cooked.

5. Return shrimp to the skillet. Add tamari, erythritol, lime juice, and fish sauce. Stir well to combine and cook for another 2 minutes.

6. Garnish with chopped peanuts, green onions, and cilantro.

INGREDIENTS:

• 1 lb (450 g) shrimp, peeled and deveined
• 2 tbsp olive oil (30 ml)
• 2 cups shredded cabbage (200 g)
• 2 cloves garlic, minced (6 g)
• 2 eggs •60 ml tamari
• 2 tbsp erythritol (24 g)
• 1 tbsp lime juice •1 tbsp fish sauce
• 1/4 cup chopped peanuts (30 g, optional)
• 2 green onions, sliced (20 g)
• 1/4 cup fresh cilantro (10 g)

Nutritional Information (per 100 grams): **Calories:** 140 kcal • **Protein:** 15g • **Carbs:** 7g • **Fats:** 7g • **Fiber:** 2g

5. Zoodle Lo Mein

🍴 **4 Servings**   🕐 **20 Minutes**

Cooking Tips:
• For extra flavor, add a splash of sesame oil or a sprinkle of sesame seeds

INGREDIENTS:

- 4 cups (400 g) zucchini noodles (zoodles)
- 1 tbsp (15 ml) olive oil
- 1 cup (150 g) sliced mushrooms
- 1/2 cup (50 g) sliced bell peppers
- 1/4 cup (30 g) sliced onions
- 2 tbsp (30 ml) soy sauce or tamari
- 1 tbsp (15 ml) rice vinegar
- 1 tsp (1 g) grated ginger
- 1/2 tsp (0.5 g) garlic powder
- 2 green onions, sliced (20 g)

INSTRUCTIONS:

1. Heat olive oil in a large skillet over medium heat.

2. Add mushrooms, bell peppers, and onions. Cook until tender.

3. Add zoodles and cook for 3-4 minutes until slightly softened.

4. Stir in soy sauce, rice vinegar, ginger, and garlic powder. Cook for another 2 minutes.

5. Garnish with green onions before serving.

Nutritional Information (per 100 grams): Calories: 50 kcal • **Protein:** 2g • **Carbs:** 8g • **Fats:** 2g • **Fiber:** 2g

6. Keto Thai Green Curry

🍴 **4 Servings**   🕐 **40 Minutes**

Cooking Tips:
• If you prefer a sweeter curry, adjust with keto-friendly sweeteners like stevia or erythritol. For more heat, add sliced chili peppers or extra curry paste

INGREDIENTS:

- 400 grams chicken breast, thinly sliced
- 200 grams coconut milk (full-fat)
- 100 grams green curry paste (check for keto-friendly ingredients)
- 150 grams bell peppers, sliced
- 100 g zucchini, sliced<100 grams spinach
- 50 grams green beans, trimmed
- 30 grams olive oil or coconut oil
- 10 grams fish sauce (optional)
- 5 grams fresh basil leaves, chopped
- 5 grams fresh cilantro, chopped
- 1 gram stevia or 2 grams salt
- 1 gram black pepper

INSTRUCTIONS:

1. Slice the chicken breast thinly and chop the vegetables.

2. Heat the oil in a large skillet or wok over medium-high heat. Add the chicken slices until they are browned and cooked through about 5-7 minutes. Remove from the pan and set aside.

Add the green curry paste to the same skillet and cook for 1-2 minutes until fragrant.

3. Pour in the coconut milk, stirring to combine with the curry paste. Bring the mixture to a gentle simmer.

4. Add the bell peppers, zucchini, green beans, and spinach to the curry.

5. Cook for about 5 minutes or until the vegetables are tender.

6. Return the chicken to the skillet, stirring to coat in the curry sauce.

7. Add fish sauce (if using), basil, cilantro, stevia (if using), salt, and pepper. Adjust seasoning to taste.

Nutritional Information (per 100 grams): Calories: 145 kcal • **Protein:** 11g • **Carbs:** 3g • **Fats:** 10g • **Fiber:** 1g

7. Spicy Beef Lettuce Wraps

🍴 4 Servings 🕐 20 Minutes

Cooking Tips:
• For extra crunch, add a few chopped water chestnuts or sliced radishes.

INSTRUCTIONS:

1. Heat olive oil in a skillet over medium-high heat. Add ground beef and cook until browned.

2. Add garlic, bell peppers, and onions. Cook for 5 minutes until vegetables are tender.

3. Stir in soy sauce, sriracha, rice vinegar, and erythritol. Cook for another 2 minutes.

4. Spoon the beef mixture into lettuce leaves and serve.

INGREDIENTS:

• 1 lb (450 g) ground beef
• 2 tbsp (30 ml) olive oil
• 1/2 cup (75 g) diced bell peppers
• 1/2 cup (75 g) diced onions
• 2 cloves garlic, minced (6 g)
• 1 tbsp (15 ml) soy sauce or tamari
• 1 tbsp (15 ml) sriracha sauce
• 1 tbsp (15 ml) rice vinegar
• 1 tbsp (15 g) erythritol
• 8 large lettuce leaves (for wrapping)

Nutritional Information (per 100 grams): **Calories:** 180 kcal • **Protein:** 16g • **Carbs:** 6g • **Fats:** 11g • **Fiber:** 2g

8. Keto Chicken Satay

🍴 4 Serving 🕐 20 Minutes (Plus marinating time)

Cooking Tips:
• Soak wooden skewers in water for 30 minutes before grilling to prevent burning. Adjust the sweetness of the peanut sauce to taste.

INSTRUCTIONS:

1. Mix marinade ingredients and marinate chicken strips for at least 1 hour.

2. Thread the marinated chicken onto skewers.

3. Grill or broil the chicken for 10-15 minutes, turning occasionally, until cooked.

4. Mix all sauce ingredients in a bowl until smooth for the peanut sauce.

5. Serve chicken satay with peanut sauce.

INGREDIENTS:

• 450 g chicken breast, cut into strips
• For the marinade:
• 30 ml coconut oil
• 30 ml soy sauce or tamari
• 15 ml lime juice • 15 g erythritol
• 2 cloves garlic, minced (6 g)
• 1 tsp (1 g) grated ginger
For the peanut sauce:
• 1/2 cup (120 g) natural peanut butter
• 30 ml coconut milk
• 15 ml soy sauce or tamari
• 15 g erythritol
• 15 ml lime juice

Nutritional Information (per 100 grams): **Calories:** 220 kcal • **Protein:** 8g • **Carbs:** 6g • **Fats:** 15g • **Fiber:** 2g

CHAPTER 11

Sides & Snacks Recipes

1. Keto Cheese Crisps

🍴 4 Servings   🕙 10 Minutes

Cooking Tips:
• Keep an eye on the crisps as they bake to prevent burning. For extra flavor, try adding a pinch of cayenne pepper or chili flakes.

INGREDIENTS:

- 1 cup (100 g) shredded cheddar cheese
- 1/4 cup (25 g) grated Parmesan cheese
- 1/2 tsp (0.5 g) paprika
- 1/4 tsp (0.5 g) garlic powder
- 1/4 tsp (0.5 g) onion powder
- 1/4 tsp (0.5 g) black pepper

INSTRUCTIONS:

1. Preheat oven to 375°F (190°C).

2. Line a baking sheet with parchment paper.

3. Mix all cheeses and spices in a bowl.

4. Spoon small mixture piles onto the baking sheet, spreading them into thin circles.

5. Bake for 5-7 minutes or until crispy and golden brown.

6. Let cool before serving.

Nutritional Information (per 100 grams): **Calories:** 500 kcal • **Protein:** 28g • **Carbs:** 4g • **Fats:** 40g • **Fiber:** 0g

2. Parmesan Zucchini Chips

🍴 4 Servings   🕙 30 Minutes

Cooking Tips:
• Slice the zucchini as thinly as possible for the crispiest results. Use a mandoline slicer if available

INGREDIENTS:

- 2 medium zucchinis (400 g), sliced thinly
- 1/2 cup (50 g) grated Parmesan cheese
- 1/2 cup (50 g) almond flour
- 1/2 tsp (1 g) garlic powder
- 1/2 tsp (1 g) dried oregano
- Salt and pepper to taste
- 1 tbsp (15 ml) olive oil

INSTRUCTIONS:

1. Preheat oven to 400°F (200°C).

2. Mix Parmesan cheese, almond flour, garlic powder, oregano, salt, and pepper in a bowl.

3. Toss zucchini slices with olive oil.

4. Coat zucchini slices with the Parmesan mixture.

5. Arrange on a baking sheet in a single layer.

6. Bake for 20-25 minutes, flipping halfway through, until crispy.

Nutritional Information (per 100 grams): **Calories:** 180 kcal • **Protein:** 8g • **Carbs:** 8g • **Fats:** 14g • **Fiber:** 2g

3. Keto Mozzarella Sticks

Y | (4 Servings

(25 Minutes

Cooking Tips:
• To prevent the cheese from melting too much, freeze the mozzarella sticks for 15 minutes before coating and baking

INGREDIENTS:

• 200 g mozzarella cheese (block form, cut into sticks)
• 1/2 cup (50 g) almond flour
• 1/4 cup (25 g) grated Parmesan cheese
• 1 large egg
• 1/2 tsp (1 g) garlic powder
• 1/2 tsp (1 g) onion powder
• 1/2 tsp (1 g) dried oregano
• Salt and pepper to taste
• 1 cup (240 ml) olive oil (for frying)

INSTRUCTIONS:

1. Preheat oven to 400°F (200°C).

2. Mix almond flour, Parmesan cheese, garlic powder, onion powder, oregano, salt, and pepper in a bowl.

3. Beat the egg in a separate bowl.

4. Dip each mozzarella stick into the egg, then coat with the almond flour.

5. Place coated sticks on a baking sheet.

6. Bake for 10-15 minutes or until golden and crispy.

7. Serve immediately with marinara sauce (optional).

Nutritional Information (per 100 grams): **Calories:** 300 kcal • **Protein:** 20g • **Carbs:** 5g • **Fats:** 22g • **Fiber:** 3g

4. Avocado Fries

Y | 4 Servings

(20 Minutes

Cooking Tips:
• For extra crispiness, use a wire rack on the baking sheet to allow air circulation around the fries

INGREDIENTS:

• 2 ripe avocados (300 g), sliced into wedges
• 1/2 cup (50 g) almond flour
• 1/4 cup (25 g) grated Parmesan cheese
• 1 large egg
• 1/2 tsp (1 g) paprika
• 1/2 tsp (1 g) garlic powder
• Salt and pepper to taste
•1 cup (240 ml) olive oil (for frying)

INSTRUCTIONS:

1. Preheat oven to 425°F (220°C).

2. Mix almond flour, Parmesan cheese, paprika, garlic powder, salt, and pepper in a bowl.

3. Beat the egg in a separate bowl.

4. Dip each avocado wedge into the egg, then coat with the almond flour.

5. Place coated wedges on a baking sheet.

6. Bake for 15-20 minutes or until golden brown.

Nutritional Information (per 100 grams): **Calories:** 250 kcal • **Protein:** 5g • **Carbs:** 10g • **Fats:** 22g • **Fiber:** 7g

5. Garlic Butter Shrimp Skewers

4 Servings (8 skewers) **15 Minutes**

Cooking Tips:
• Soak wooden skewers in water for 30 minutes before grilling to prevent burning.

INGREDIENTS:

• 500 g large shrimp, peeled and deveined
• 3 tbsp (45 g) unsalted butter
• 4 cloves garlic, minced
• 1 tbsp (15 ml) lemon juice
• 1/4 cup (15 g) fresh parsley, chopped
• 1/2 tsp (1 g) paprika
• Salt and pepper to taste

INSTRUCTIONS:

1. Preheat grill or broiler to medium-high heat.

2. Melt butter in a pan over medium heat. Add garlic and cook for 1-2 minutes until fragrant.

3. Remove from heat and stir in lemon juice, parsley, paprika, salt, and pepper.

4. Thread shrimp onto skewers.

5. Brush shrimp with the garlic butter mixture.

6. Grill or broil for 2-3 minutes per side or until shrimp are pink and opaque.

Nutritional Information (per 100 grams): **Calories:** 150 kcal • **Protein:** 25g • **Carbs:** 1g • **Fats:** 6g • **Fiber:** 0g

6. Keto Onion Rings

4 Servings **20 Minutes**

Cooking Tips:
• For less mess, use a deep fryer if available. Make sure the oil is hot before frying to keep the onion rings crispy

INGREDIENTS:

• 2 large onions, sliced into rings (about 300 g)
• 1 cup (120 g) almond flour
• 1/2 cup (50 g) grated Parmesan cheese
• 2 large eggs
• 1/2 tsp (1 g) paprika
• 1/2 tsp (1 g) garlic powder
• Salt and pepper to taste
• 1 cup (240 ml) olive oil for frying

INSTRUCTIONS:

1. Heat olive oil in a large skillet over medium-high heat.

2. Mix almond flour, Parmesan cheese, paprika, garlic powder, salt, and pepper in one bowl.

3. In another bowl, beat eggs.

4. Dip onion rings in eggs, then coat with the almond flour.

5. Fry onion rings in batches until golden brown, about 2-3 minutes per side. Drain on paper towels.

Nutritional Information (per 100 grams): **Calories:** 200 kcal • **Protein:** 7g • **Carbs:** 10g • **Fats:** 15g • **Fiber:** 4g

CHAPTER 12

Desserts & Sweet Treats Recipes

1. Almond Flour Brownies

🍴 4 Servings   🕐 25 Minutes

Cooking Tips:
• *Ensure the butter is fully melted before mixing with erythritol to avoid clumps. Let the brownies cool completely before cutting to firm up*

INGREDIENTS:

• Almond flour: 120 grams
• Cocoa powder: 30 grams
• Erythritol: 50 grams
• Eggs: 3 large (150 grams)
• Unsalted butter: 80 grams
• Vanilla extract: 5 ml (4 grams)
• Baking powder: 1/2 tsp (2 grams)

INSTRUCTIONS:

1. Preheat oven to 175°C (350°F) and line a baking pan with parchment paper.

2. Melt the butter and mix with erythritol.

3. Add eggs and vanilla extract, mixing well.

4. Stir in almond flour, cocoa powder, and baking powder until smooth.

5. Pour the batter into the pan and bake for 20-25 minutes or until a toothpick comes out clean.

Nutritional Information (per 100 grams): **Calories:** 350 kcal • **Protein:** 10g • **Carbs:** 8g • **Fats:** 32g • **Fiber:** 4g

2. Keto Cheesecake Bites

🍴 4 Servings   🕐 15 Minutes

Cooking Tips:
• *Use room temperature cream cheese for a smoother filling. For added flavor, you can incorporate a few drops of lemon zest.*

INGREDIENTS:

• Cream cheese: 225 grams
• Erythritol: 30 grams
• Vanilla extract: 5 ml (4 grams)
• Lemon juice: 10 ml (8 grams)
• Almond flour: 20 grams (for crust)
• Unsalted butter: 30 grams (for crust)

INSTRUCTIONS:

1. Preheat oven to 175°C (350°F). Mix almond flour with melted butter and press into mini muffin cups.

2. Bake crust for 5 minutes and let cool.

3. Blend cream cheese, erythritol, vanilla extract, and lemon juice until smooth.

4. Spoon the filling onto the cooled crusts and refrigerate for at least 2 hours.

Nutritional Information (per 100 grams): **Calories:** 360 kcal • **Protein:** 6g • **Carbs:** 4g • **Fats:** 34g • **Fiber:** 2g

3. Coconut Fat Bombs

🍴 **2 Servings**

🕐 **10 Minutes** plus chilling

Cooking Tips:
• *Ensure the coconut oil is completely melted before mixing to prevent clumps. Store in the fridge or freezer to maintain firmness.*

INSTRUCTIONS:

1. Melt coconut oil and mix with erythritol and vanilla extract.

2. Stir in shredded coconut until well combined.

3. Spoon mixture into silicone molds and refrigerate until solidified.

INGREDIENTS:

• Shredded unsweetened coconut: 100 grams
• Coconut oil: 60 grams
• Erythritol: 20 grams
• Vanilla extract: 5 ml (4 grams)

Nutritional Information (per 100 grams): **Calories:** 580 kcal • **Protein:** 2g • **Carbs:** 6g • **Fats:** 60g • **Fiber:** 5g

4. Keto Lemon Bars

🍴 **2 Servings**

🕐 **30 Minutes**

Cooking Tips:
• *Use fresh lemon juice for the best flavor. Ensure the bars are completely cooled before cutting to avoid crumbling.*

INSTRUCTIONS:

1. Preheat oven to 175°C (350°F). Mix almond flour with erythritol and melted butter. Press into a baking pan.

2. Bake for 10 minutes until lightly golden.

3. For the filling, whisk eggs, lemon juice, lemon zest, erythritol, and baking powder.

4. Pour over the pre-baked crust and bake for 15-20 minutes or until set.

5. Let cool before cutting into bars

INGREDIENTS:

• Almond flour: 150 grams
• Erythritol: 50 grams
• Unsalted butter: 60 grams
• Eggs: 3 large (150 grams)
• Lemon juice: 60 ml (50 grams)
• Lemon zest: 10 grams
• Baking powder: 1/2 tsp (2 grams)

Nutritional Information (per 100 grams): **Calories:** 320 kcal • **Protein:** 7g • **Carbs:** 10g • **Fats:** 28g • **Fiber:** 3g

5. Raspberry Cream Cheese Bars

🍴 3 Servings　　🕐 30 Minutes

Cooking Tips:
• Use room temperature cream cheese for a smoother filling. Ensure the bars are fully cooled for cleaner cuts

INGREDIENTS:

- Almond flour: 150 grams
- Erythritol: 60 grams
- Unsalted butter: 60 grams
- Cream cheese: 200 grams
- Fresh raspberries: 100 grams
- Egg: 1 large (50 grams)
- Vanilla extract: 5 ml (4 grams)
- Baking powder: 1/2 tsp (2 grams)

INSTRUCTIONS:

1. Preheat oven to 175°C (350°F). Line an 8x8-inch baking pan with parchment paper.

2. Mix almond flour, erythritol, and melted butter. Press into the bottom of the pan.

3. Bake the crust for 10 minutes and let it cool.

4. Blend cream cheese with erythritol, egg, and vanilla extract until smooth.

5. Spread the cream cheese mixture over the cooled crust.

6. Dot with raspberries and bake for 20 minutes or until set.

7. Cool completely before cutting into bars

Nutritional Information (per 100 grams): **Calories:** 320 kcal • **Protein:** 6g • **Carbs:** 11g • **Fats:** 27g • **Fiber:** 3g

6. Pecan Pie Bars

🍴 4 Servings　　🕐 40 Minutes

Cooking Tips:
• Ensure the filling is evenly distributed over the crust. Let the bars cool fully before slicing to prevent crumbling

INGREDIENTS:

For the Crust:
- Almond flour: 150 grams
- Unsalted butter, melted: 75 grams
- Erythritol: 30 grams

For the Filling:
- Pecans, chopped: 150 grams
- Eggs: 2 large (100 grams)
- Erythritol: 80 grams
- Unsalted butter: 60 grams
- Vanilla extract: 5 ml (4 grams)
- Salt: 1/4 tsp (1 gram

INSTRUCTIONS:

1. Preheat oven to 175°C (350°F). Line an 8x8-inch baking pan with parchment paper.

2. Mix almond flour, melted butter, and erythritol. Press into the bottom of the prepared pan.

3. Bake the crust for 10 minutes and let it cool slightly.

4. For the filling, melt butter and mix with erythritol, eggs, vanilla extract, and salt.

5. Stir in chopped pecans. Pour the mixture over the pre-baked crust.

6. Bake for 25-30 minutes until the filling is set and the top is golden.

7. Cool completely before cutting into bars.

Nutritional Information (per 100 grams): **Calories:** 400 kcal • **Protein:** 8g • **Carbs:** 14g • **Fats:** 35g • **Fiber:** 4g

7. Keto Strawberry Shortcake

4 Servings   **30 Minutes**

INGREDIENTS:

For the Cake:
• Almond flour: 150 grams
• Baking powder: 1 tsp (4 grams)
• Erythritol: 50 grams
• Eggs: 3 large (150 grams)
• Unsalted butter, melted: 60 grams
• Vanilla extract: 5 ml (4 grams)
For the Topping:
• Fresh strawberries, sliced: 200 grams
• Erythritol: 20 grams
• Heavy cream: 200 ml (200 grams)

INSTRUCTIONS:

1. Preheat oven to 175°C (350°F). Grease and line a cake pan.

2. Mix almond flour, baking powder, erythritol, eggs, melted butter, and vanilla extract.

3. Pour batter into the prepared pan and bake for 20-25 minutes until golden brown and a toothpick comes out clean.

4. Allow the cake to cool, then slice it into four portions.

5. Mix strawberries with erythritol. Whip heavy cream until stiff peaks form.

6. Top each cake slice with strawberries and whipped cream.

Nutritional Information (per 100 grams): **Calories:** 290 kcal • **Protein:** 6g • **Carbs:** 15g • **Fats:** 25g • **Fiber:** 4g

8. Keto Chocolate Truffles

4 Serving   **20 Minutes (Plus chilling time)**

INGREDIENTS:

• Unsweetened cocoa powder: 50 grams
• Heavy cream: 100 ml (100 grams)
• Unsweetened dark chocolate (85% cocoa), chopped: 100 grams
• Erythritol: 30 grams
• Vanilla extract: 1 tsp (5 ml, 4 grams)

INSTRUCTIONS:

1. Heat the heavy cream in a saucepan over medium heat until it begins to simmer.

2. Remove from heat and add the chopped dark chocolate. Stir until melted and smooth.

3. Stir in erythritol and vanilla extract until well combined.

4. Chill the mixture in the refrigerator for 30 minutes until firm.

5. Once firm, scoop out small portions and roll into balls.

6. Roll the truffles in additional cocoa powder if desired.

7. Store in an airtight container in the refrigerator.

Nutritional Information (per 100 grams): **Calories:** 430 kcal • **Protein:** 5g • **Carbs:** 14g • **Fats:** 38g • **Fiber:** 8g

9. Pumpkin Spice Muffins

4 Servings   **25 Minutes**

Cooking Tips:
• Ensure the muffins are fully cooled before storing to prevent sogginess. For extra flavor, sprinkle a bit of additional pumpkin spice on top before baking.

INGREDIENTS:

• Almond flour: 200 grams
• Pumpkin puree: 100 grams
• Eggs: 3 large (150 grams)
• Erythritol: 80 grams
• Baking powder: 1 tsp (4 grams)
• Pumpkin spice: 2 tsp (4 grams)
• Vanilla extract: 1 tsp (5 ml, 4 grams)
• Unsalted butter, melted: 60 grams

INSTRUCTIONS:

1. Preheat oven to 175°C (350°F). Line a muffin tin with paper liners.

2. Mix almond flour, erythritol, baking powder, and pumpkin spice in a bowl.

3. Whisk together the eggs, pumpkin puree, melted butter, and vanilla extract in another bowl.

4. Combine the wet and dry ingredients, mixing until smooth.

5. Divide the batter evenly among the muffin cups.

6. Bake for 20-25 minutes until a toothpick inserted into the center comes clean.

7. Cool on a wire rack before serving.

Nutritional Information (per 100 grams): **Calories:** 320 kcal • **Protein:** 8g • **Carbs:** 10g • **Fats:** 27g • **Fiber:** 5g

10. Keto Apple Pie

8 Servings   **50 Minutes**

Cooking Tips:
• To prevent a soggy crust, ensure the apples are well-drained before adding to the crust. Serve with a dollop of whipped cream or a scoop of keto ice cream for added indulgence.

INGREDIENTS:

• Almond flour: 200 grams
• Coconut flour: 30 grams
• Erythritol: 50 grams
• Unsalted butter, melted: 100 grams
• Egg: 1 large (50 grams)
For the Filling:
• Granny Smith apples, peeled and thinly sliced: 300 grams
• Erythritol: 60 grams
• Cinnamon: 1 tsp (2 grams)
• Nutmeg: 1/4 tsp (0.5 grams)
• Lemon juice: 1 tbsp (15 ml,/grams)

INSTRUCTIONS:

1. Preheat oven to 175°C (350°F). Grease a pie dish.

2. Mix almond flour, coconut flour, erythritol, melted butter, and egg for the crust until a dough forms. Press into the bottom and sides of the pie dish.

3. Bake the crust for 10 minutes.

4. For the filling, toss apple slices with erythritol, cinnamon, nutmeg, and lemon juice.

5. Pour the apple mixture into the pre-baked crust.

6. Bake for 35-40 minutes until the filling is bubbly and the crust is golden brown.

7. Cool before serving

Nutritional Information (per 100 grams): **Calories:** 320 kcal • **Protein:** 6g • **Carbs:** 18g • **Fats:** 24g • **Fiber:** 5g

CHAPTER 13

Bread Recipes

1. Almond Flour Bread

🍴 1 loaf
(about 10 slices)

🕐 45 Minutes

Cooking Tips:
• For a crustier crust, you can bake the bread on a baking sheet instead of a loaf pan

INGREDIENTS:

• Almond flour: 200 grams
• Baking powder: 1 tsp (4 grams)
• Salt: 1/2 tsp (2 grams)
• Eggs: 4 large (200 grams)
• Unsalted butter, melted: 60 grams
• Apple cider vinegar: 1 tbsp (15 ml)
• Water: 60 ml (60 grams)

INSTRUCTIONS:

1. Preheat the oven to 180°C (350°F). Grease and line a loaf pan.

2. Combine almond flour, baking powder, and salt in a large bowl.

3. Whisk together the eggs, melted butter, apple cider vinegar, and water in another bowl.

4. Mix the wet ingredients into the dry ingredients until well combined.

5. Pour the batter into the prepared loaf pan and smooth the top.

6. Bake for 40-45 minutes or until a toothpick inserted into the center comes clean.

7. Let the bread cool in the pan for 10 minutes before transferring to a wire rack to cool completely.

Nutritional Information (per 100 grams): **Calories:** 320 kcal • **Protein:** 12g • **Carbs:** 8g • **Fats:** 28g • **Fiber:** 6g

2. Cheddar Garlic Biscuits

🍴 2 Biscuits

🕐 25 Minutes

Cooking Tips:
• For extra flavor, brush the biscuits with melted butter and sprinkle with additional garlic powder right after baking.

INGREDIENTS:

• Almond flour: 180 grams
• Baking powder: 1 tbsp (12 grams)
• Salt: 1/2 tsp (2 grams)
• Eggs: 2 large (100 grams)
• Shredded cheddar cheese: 100 grams
• Garlic powder: 1 tsp (3 grams)
• Unsalted butter, melted: 60 grams

INSTRUCTIONS:

1. Preheat the oven to 200°C (400°F). Line a baking sheet with parchment paper.

2. Mix almond flour, baking powder, salt, and garlic powder in a bowl.

3. In another bowl, whisk together the eggs and melted butter.

4. Add the wet ingredients to the dry ingredients and mix until combined.

5. Fold in the shredded cheddar cheese.

6. Drop spoonfuls of dough onto the baking sheet, forming eight biscuits.

7. Bake for 15-20 minutes, or until golden brown.

8. Cool slightly before serving.

Nutritional Information (per 100 grams): **Calories:** 330 kcal • **Protein:** 14g • **Carbs:** 6g • **Fats:** 28g • **Fiber:** 4g

3. Flaxseed Bread

🍴   🕐

1 loaf
(about 12 slices)   50 Minutes

Cooking Tips:
• For a crustier bread, bake it on a baking sheet instead of a loaf pan. Ensure it is completely cool before slicing to avoid crumbling.

INGREDIENTS:

• Ground flaxseeds: 200 grams
• Baking powder: 1 tbsp (12 grams)
• Salt: 1/2 tsp (2 grams)
• Eggs: 4 large (200 grams)
• Unsalted butter, melted: 60 grams
• Water: 60 ml (60 grams)

INSTRUCTIONS:

1. Preheat the oven to 180°C (350°F). Grease and line a loaf pan.

2. Mix ground flaxseeds, baking powder, and salt in a bowl.

3. Whisk together the eggs, melted butter, and water in another bowl.

4. Combine the wet and dry ingredients until well-mixed.

5. Pour the batter into the prepared loaf pan and smooth the top.

6. Bake for 45-50 minutes or until a toothpick inserted into the center comes clean.

7. Cool in the pan for 10 minutes before transferring to a wire rack to cool completely.

Nutritional Information (per 100 grams): **Calories:** 340 kcal • **Protein:** 12g • **Carbs:** 8g • **Fats:** 30g • **Fiber:** 16g

AL

4. Herb and Cheese Bread

🍴   🕐

1 loaf
(about 12 slices)   45 Minutes

Cooking Tips:
• For extra flavor, add fresh herbs like rosemary or thyme. Make sure to mix well to evenly distribute the cheese.

INSTRUCTIONS:

1. Preheat the oven to 180°C (350°F). Grease and line a loaf pan.

2. Mix almond flour, baking powder, salt, and dried herbs in a bowl.

3. Whisk together eggs, melted butter, and sour cream in another bowl.4. Combine wet and dry ingredients until smooth. Fold in shredded cheese.

5. Pour the batter into the prepared loaf pan.

6. Bake for 40-45 minutes or until golden brown and a toothpick inserted into the center comes out clean.

7. Cool in the pan for 10 minutes before transferring to a wire rack to cool completely.

INGREDIENTS:

• Almond flour: 200 grams
• Baking powder: 1 tbsp (12 grams)
• Salt: 1/2 tsp (2 grams)
• Dried Italian herbs: 1 tbsp (2 grams)
• Shredded cheddar cheese: 100 grams
• Eggs: 4 large (200 grams)
• Unsalted butter, melted: 60 grams
• Sour cream: 60 grams)

Nutritional Information (per 100 grams): **Calories:** 340 kcal • **Protein:** 13g • **Carbs:** 6g • **Fats:** 28g • **Fiber:** 4g

5. Zucchini Bread

🍴 **1 loaf**
(about 12 slices)

🕐 **50 Minutes**

INGREDIENTS:

• Almond flour: 180 grams
• Baking powder: 1 tsp (4 grams)
• Salt: 1/2 tsp (2 grams)
• Ground cinnamon: 1 tsp (2 grams)
• Eggs: 3 large (150 grams)
• Zucchini, grated: 150 grams
• Unsalted butter, melted: 60 grams
• Erythritol or another keto-friendly sweetener: 60 grams (optional)

INSTRUCTIONS:

1. Preheat the oven to 180°C (350°F). Grease and line a loaf pan.

2. Mix almond flour, baking powder, salt, and cinnamon in a bowl.

3. In another bowl, whisk together eggs, melted butter, and sweetener (if using).

4. Stir in the grated zucchini.

5. Combine wet and dry ingredients until smooth.

6. Pour the batter into the prepared loaf pan.

7. Bake for 45-50 minutes or until a toothpick inserted into the center comes clean.

8. Cool in the pan for 10 minutes before transferring to a wire rack to cool completely

Nutritional Information (per 100 grams): Calories: 290 kcal • **Protein:** 10g • **Carbs:** 8g • **Fats:** 24g • **Fiber:** 5g

6. Cauliflower Breadsticks

🍴 **4 Servings**

🕐 **30 Minutes**

INGREDIENTS:

• Cauliflower florets: 500 grams
• Almond flour: 60 grams
• Egg: 1 large (50 grams)
• Shredded mozzarella cheese: 100 grams
• Garlic powder: 1 tsp (3 grams)
• Dried oregano: 1/2 tsp (1 gram)
• Salt: 1/2 tsp (2 grams)

INSTRUCTIONS:

1. Preheat the oven to 220°C (425°F). Line a baking sheet with parchment paper.

2. Steam or microwave the cauliflower florets until tender. Drain well, and pat dry with a paper towel.

3. Process the cauliflower in a food processor until finely chopped. Mix in almond flour, egg, mozzarella cheese, garlic powder, oregano, and salt.

4. Spread the mixture evenly on the prepared baking sheet, forming a rectangular shape.

5. Bake for 20-25 minutes or until golden brown and crispy.

Nutritional Information (per 100 grams): Calories: 190 kcal • **Protein:** 9g • **Carbs:** 8g • **Fats:** 13g • **Fiber:** 4g

BONUS CHAPTER

Sauces & Dressing Recipes

1. Keto Alfredo Sauce

INGREDIENTS:

- Unsalted butter: 60 grams
- Heavy cream: 240 ml
- Garlic, minced: 2 cloves (6 grams)
- Grated Parmesan cheese: 100 grams
- Salt: 1/2 tsp (2 grams)
- Black pepper: 1/4 tsp (1 gram)
- Nutmeg (optional): 1/4 tsp (0.5 grams)

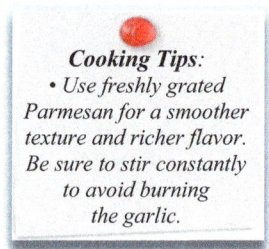

Cooking Tips:
- *Use freshly grated Parmesan for a smoother texture and richer flavor. Be sure to stir constantly to avoid burning the garlic.*

INSTRUCTIONS:

1. In a saucepan, melt butter over medium heat. 2. Add minced garlic and sauté for 1 minute until fragrant.
3. Pour in the heavy cream, stirring constantly. 4. Bring the mixture to a simmer and reduce heat to low.
5. Gradually whisk in the Parmesan cheese until thoroughly melted and the sauce is smooth.
6. Season with salt, pepper, and nutmeg (if using). Simmer for another 2-3 minutes.
7. Remove from heat and serve immediately over your favorite keto pasta or dish.

Nutritional Information (per 100 grams): **Calories:** 240 kcal • **Protein:** 6g • **Carbohydrates:** 2g • **Fats:** 23g • **Fiber:** 0g

2. Avocado Lime Dressing

INGREDIENTS:

- Ripe avocado: 1 medium (150 grams)
- Fresh lime juice: 2 tbsp (30 ml)
- Olive oil: 2 tbsp (30 ml)
- Greek yogurt (full-fat): 60 grams
- Garlic powder: 1/2 tsp (1 gram)
- Salt: 1/4 tsp (1 gram)
- Black pepper: 1/4 tsp (1 gram)
- Fresh cilantro (optional): 2 tbsp (6 grams), chopped

Cooking Tips:
- *For a thinner dressing, add a bit of water or extra lime juice. This dressing can be stored in the refrigerator for up to 3 days.*

INSTRUCTIONS:

1. Scoop the avocado into a blender or food processor.
2. Add lime juice, olive oil, Greek yogurt, garlic powder, salt, and pepper.
3. Blend until smooth and creamy.
4. Stir in chopped cilantro if desired.
5. Adjust seasoning to taste and serve chilled.

Nutritional Information (per 100 grams): **Calories:** 210 kcal • **Protein:** 3g • **Carbohydrates:** 5g • **Fats:** 20g • **Fiber:** 4g

3. Keto BBQ Sauce

INGREDIENTS:

- Tomato paste: 120 grams
- Apple cider vinegar: 1/4 cup (60 ml)
- Water: 1/4 cup (60 ml)
- Erythritol: 3 tbsp (24 grams)
- Worcestershire sauce: 2 tbsp (30 ml)
- Smoked paprika: 1 tsp (2 grams)
- Garlic powder: 1/2 tsp (1 gram)
- Onion powder: 1/2 tsp (1 gram)
- Salt: 1/4 tsp (1 gram)
- Black pepper: 1/4 tsp (1 gram)

Cooking Tips:
- *This sauce can be stored in an airtight container in the refrigerator for up to 2 weeks.*

INSTRUCTIONS:

1. Combine all ingredients in a saucepan over medium heat.
2. Stir until erythritol is dissolved and the mixture begins to simmer.
3. Reduce heat and simmer for 15 minutes, stirring occasionally until thickening.
4. Remove from heat and let cool before using.

Nutritional Information (per 100 grams): **Calories:** 80 kcal • **Protein:** 2g • **Carbohydrates:** 7g • **Fats:** 2g • **Fiber:** 2g

4. Ranch Dressing

INGREDIENTS:

- Mayonnaise (full-fat):120 grams
- Sour cream (full-fat): 120 grams
- Fresh chives: 6 grams, chopped
- Fresh parsley:6 grams, chopped
- Garlic powder: 1/2 tsp (1 gram)
- Onion powder: 1/2 tsp (1 gram)
- Salt: 1/2 tsp (2 grams)
- Black pepper: 1/4 tsp (1 gram)
- Lemon juice: 1 tbsp (15 ml)

Cooking Tips:
Use fresh herbs for the best flavor. This dressing will keep in the refrigerator for up to 1 week.

INSTRUCTIONS:

1. In a bowl, combine mayonnaise and sour cream.
2. Add chopped chives, parsley, garlic powder, onion powder, salt, pepper, and lemon juice.
3. Mix until well combined and creamy.
4. Chill in the refrigerator for at least 30 minutes to allow flavors to meld.

Nutritional Information (per 100 grams): **Calories:** 320 kcal • **Protein:** 2g • **Carbohydrates:** 3g • **Fats:** 32g • **Fiber:** 1g

5. Keto Marinara Sauce

INGREDIENTS:

- Canned crushed tomatoes: 400 grams
- Olive oil: 2 tbsp (30 ml)
- Garlic, minced: 3 cloves (9 grams)
- Dried oregano: 1 tsp (1 gram)
- Salt: 1/2 tsp (2 grams)
- Black pepper: 1/4 tsp (1 gram)
- Red pepper flakes (optional): 1/4 tsp
- Fresh basil (optional): 2 tbsp (6 grams), chopped

Cooking Tips:
• For a smoother sauce, use an immersion blender to blend until smooth. This sauce can be stored in the refrigerator for up to 1 week or frozen for up to 3 months

INSTRUCTIONS:

1. Heat olive oil in a saucepan over medium heat.
2. Add minced garlic and cook for 1 minute until fragrant.
3. Add crushed tomatoes, oregano, basil, salt, pepper, and red pepper flakes (if using).
4. Simmer for 20-25 minutes, stirring occasionally, until the sauce thickens.
5. Stir in fresh basil if desired before serving.

Nutritional Information (per 100 grams): **Calories:** 80 kcal • **Protein:** 2g • **Carbohydrates:** 6g • **Fats:** 6g • **Fiber:** 2g

6. Blue Cheese Dressing

INGREDIENTS:

- Blue cheese, crumbled: 100 grams
- Mayonnaise (full-fat): 120 grams
- Sour cream (full-fat): 120 grams
- Lemon juice: 1 tbsp (15 ml)
- Blue cheese, crumbled: 100 grams
- Mayonnaise (full-fat): 120 grams
- Sour cream (full-fat): 120 grams
- Lemon juice: 1 tbsp (15 ml)

Cooking Tips:
• For a smoother dressing, mash the blue cheese with a fork before mixing. Adjust seasoning to taste.

INSTRUCTIONS:

1. In a bowl, combine the mayonnaise and sour cream.
2. Stir in the crumbled blue cheese, lemon juice, garlic powder, salt, and pepper.
3. Mix until well combined.
4. Refrigerate for at least 30 minutes to let the flavors meld.
5. Garnish with fresh chives if desired before serving.

Nutritional Information (per 100 grams): **Calories:** 250 kcal • **Protein:** 5g • **Carbohydrates:** 4g • **Fats:** 24g • **Fiber:** 0g

7. Keto Pesto Sauce

INGREDIENTS:

- Fresh basil leaves: 1 cup (30 grams)
- Pine nuts: 1/4 cup (30 grams)
- Parmesan cheese, grated: 1/2 cup (50 grams)
- Garlic, minced: 2 cloves (6 grams)
- Olive oil: 1/2 cup (120 ml)
- Lemon juice: 1 tbsp (15 ml)
- Salt: 1/4 tsp (1 gram)
- Black pepper: 1/4 tsp (1 gram)

Cooking Tips: Toasting the pine nuts before adding them to the pesto enhances their flavor. For a nut-free version, use sunflower seeds.

INSTRUCTIONS:

1. Combine basil leaves, pine nuts, Parmesan cheese, and minced garlic in a food processor.
2. Pulse until finely chopped.
3. With the processor running, slowly stream the olive oil until the mixture is smooth.
4. Add lemon juice, salt, and pepper. Blend until thoroughly combined. 5. Store in an airtight container in the refrigerator for up to 1 week.

Nutritional Information (per 100 grams): **Calories:** 450 kcal • **Protein:** 10g • **Carbohydrates:** 6g • **Fats:** 43g • **Fiber:** 2g

8. Lemon Butter Sauce

INGREDIENTS:

- Unsalted butter: 100 grams
- Fresh lemon juice: 1/4 cup (60 ml)
- Garlic, minced: 2 cloves (6 grams)
- Fresh parsley, chopped: 2 tbsp (6 grams)
- Salt: 1/2 tsp (2 grams)
- Black pepper: 1/4 tsp (1 gram)

Cooking Tips:
• For extra richness, add a splash of white wine or a pinch of cayenne pepper. Keep the sauce warm until serving to maintain its consistency.

INSTRUCTIONS:

1. In a saucepan, melt the butter over medium heat.
2. Add minced garlic and cook for 1 minute until fragrant.
3. Stir in lemon juice and simmer for 2 minutes.
4. Remove from heat and stir in chopped parsley, salt, and pepper.
5. Serve warm over seafood, vegetables, or chicken.

Nutritional Information (per 100 grams): **Calories:** 740 kcal • **Protein:** 1g • **Carbohydrates:** 1g • **Fats:** 80g • **Fiber:** 0g

9. Caesar Dressing

INGREDIENTS:

- Mayonnaise (full-fat): 120 grams
- Parmesan cheese, grated: 25 grams
- Lemon juice: 2 tbsp (30 ml)
- Dijon mustard: 1 tsp (5 grams)
- Worcestershire sauce: 1 tsp (5 ml
- Garlic powder: 1/2 tsp (1 gram)
- Anchovy paste: 1 tsp (5 grams)
- Salt: 1/4 tsp (1 gram)
- Black pepper: 1/4 tsp (1 gram)

Cooking Tips:
• If you prefer a creamier texture, blend the ingredients in a food processor. The dressing can be stored in the refrigerator for up to 1 week.

INSTRUCTIONS:

1. Combine mayonnaise, Parmesan cheese, lemon juice, Dijon mustard, Worcestershire sauce, garlic powder, and anchovy paste in a bowl.
2. Whisk until smooth and well combined.
3. Season with salt and pepper to taste.
4. Refrigerate for at least 30 minutes to let flavors meld.

Nutritional Information (per 100 grams): **Calories:** 300 kcal • **Protein:** 5g • **Carbohydrates:** 2g • **Fats:** 29g • **Fiber:** 0g

10. Keto Mayonnaise

INGREDIENTS:

- Egg yolks: 2 large (40 grams)
- Dijon mustard: 1 tbsp (15 grams)
- Lemon juice: 2 tbsp (30 ml)
- Olive oil: 1 cup (240 ml)
- Salt: 1/2 tsp (2 grams)
- Black pepper: 1/4 tsp (1 gram)

Cooking Tips:
• Use room temperature eggs and oil for easier emulsification. For a tangier flavor, adjust the amount of lemon juice or mustard.

INSTRUCTIONS:

1. Combine egg yolks, Dijon mustard, and lemon juice in a bowl or food processor.2. With the processor running, slowly drizzle in the olive oil until the mixture emulsifies and thickens.
3. Season with salt and pepper.
4. Store in an airtight container in the refrigerator for up to 1 week.

Nutritional Information (per 100 grams): **Calories:** 700 kcal • **Protein:** 6g • **Carbohydrates:** 1g • **Fats:** 72g • **Fiber:** 0g

11. Buffalo Sauce

INGREDIENTS:

- Hot sauce (e.g., Frank's RedHot): 1/2 cup (120 ml)
- Unsalted butter: 1/4 cup (56 grams)
- White vinegar: 1 tbsp (15 ml)
- Garlic powder: 1/2 tsp (1 gram)
- Paprika: 1/2 tsp (1 gram)
- Salt: 1/4 tsp (1 gram)

Cooking Tips:
• Adjust the amount of hot sauce for more or less heat. For a thicker sauce, add more butter.

INSTRUCTIONS:

1. In a saucepan, melt the butter over medium heat.
2. Stir in the hot sauce, white vinegar, garlic powder, paprika, and salt.
3. Simmer for 2-3 minutes, stirring frequently, until well combined.
4. Remove from heat and let cool slightly before using.

Nutritional Information (per 100 grams): **Calories:** 290 kcal • **Protein:** 0,5g • **Carbohydrates:** 1g • **Fats:** 31g • **Fiber:** 0g

12. Keto Hollandaise Sauce

INGREDIENTS:

- Egg yolks: 3 large (60 grams)
- Unsalted butter: 1/2 cup (113 grams), melted
- Lemon juice: 2 tbsp (30 ml)
- Dijon mustard: 1 tsp (5 grams)
- Salt: 1/2 tsp (2 grams)
- Black pepper: 1/4 tsp (1 gram)

Cooking Tips:
• Ensure that the bowl doesn't touch the simmering water to prevent scrambling the eggs. Serve immediately or keep warm in a double boiler.

INSTRUCTIONS:

1. In a heatproof bowl, whisk egg yolks and lemon juice.
2. Place the bowl over a pot of simmering water (double boiler method), whisking continuously.
3. Gradually drizzle the melted butter while whisking until the sauce thickens.
4. Stir in Dijon mustard, salt, and pepper.
5. Remove from heat and serve warm.

Nutritional Information (per 100 grams): **Calories:** 600 kcal • **Protein:** 6g • **Carbohydrates:** 2g • **Fats:** 64g • **Fiber:** 0g

13. Creamy Garlic Dressing

INGREDIENTS:

- Mayonnaise (full-fat):120 grams
- Sour cream (full-fat): 120 grams
- Garlic cloves, minced: 3 cloves
- Lemon juice: 2 tbsp (30 ml)
- Dried dill: 1 tsp (1 gram)
- Salt: 1/4 tsp (1 gram)
- Black pepper: 1/4 tsp (1 gram)

Cooking Tips:
For a milder garlic flavor, use roasted garlic instead of raw. Adjust the garlic amount based on your taste preference.

INSTRUCTIONS:

1. In a bowl, mix mayonnaise and sour cream.
2. Stir in minced garlic, lemon juice, dried dill, salt, and pepper.
3. Refrigerate for at least 30 minutes to let the flavors meld.
4. Stir before serving.

Nutritional Information (per 100 grams): **Calories:** 350 kcal • **Protein:** 4g • **Carbohydrates:** 4g • **Fats:** 35g • **Fiber:** 0g

14. Keto Teriyaki Sauce

INGREDIENTS:

- Soy sauce (or coconut aminos for less sodium): 1/2 cup (120 ml)
- Water: 1/4 cup (60 ml)
- Erythritol: 1/4 cup (50 grams)
- Apple cider vinegar: 2 tbsp (30 ml)
- Garlic, minced: 2 cloves (6 grams)
- Fresh ginger, grated: 1 tbsp (6 grams
- Xantham gum: 1/2 tsp (1 gram)

Cooking Tips:
• Adjust sweetness or tanginess to taste by modifying erythritol or vinegar. For a thicker sauce, increase the xantham gum slightly.

INSTRUCTIONS:

1. Combine soy sauce, water, erythritol, apple cider vinegar, garlic, and ginger in a saucepan.
2. Bring to a simmer over medium heat, stirring occasionally.
3. Sprinkle in the xantham gum while whisking to thicken the sauce.
4. Simmer for an additional 2-3 minutes until thickened.
5. Let cool before using.

Nutritional Information (per 100 grams): **Calories:** 50 kcal • **Protein:** 2g • **Carbohydrates:** 6g • **Fats:** 0g • **Fiber:** 0g

15. Chipotle Mayo

INGREDIENTS:

- Mayonnaise (full-fat): 1/2 cup (120 grams)
- Chipotle peppers in adobo sauce: 2 peppers (15 grams), finely chopped
- Lime juice: 1 tbsp (15 ml)
- Garlic powder: 1/2 tsp (1 gram)
- Salt: 1/4 tsp (1 gram)
- Black pepper: 1/4 tsp (1 gram)

Cooking Tips:
• For a spicier kick, add more chipotle peppers or a splash of the adobo sauce. Store in the refrigerator for up to 1 week.

INSTRUCTIONS:

1. In a bowl, combine mayonnaise and chopped chipotle peppers.
2. Stir in lime juice, garlic powder, salt, and pepper.
3. Mix until smooth and well combined.
4. Refrigerate for at least 30 minutes to allow the flavors to meld.

Nutritional Information (per 100 grams): **Calories:** 350 kcal • **Protein:** 2g • **Carbohydrates:** 4g • **Fats:** 35g • **Fiber:** 1g

16. Keto Tartar Sauce

INGREDIENTS:

- Mayonnaise (full-fat): 1/2 cup (120 grams)
- Dill pickle relish (sugar-free): 1/4 cup (60 grams)
- Lemon juice: 1 tbsp (15 ml)
- Fresh dill, chopped: 1 tbsp (2 grams)
- Capers, chopped: 1 tbsp (8 grams)
- Salt: 1/4 tsp (1 gram)
- Black pepper: 1/4 tsp (1 gram)

Cooking Tips:
Use sugar-free relish to keep the recipe keto-friendly. Adjust the amount of dill and capers according to your taste preference.

INSTRUCTIONS:

1. Combine mayonnaise, dill pickle relish, lemon juice, fresh dill, and capers in a bowl.
2. Mix until well combined.
3. Season with salt and pepper.
4. Chill in the refrigerator for at least 30 minutes before serving to allow flavors to meld.

Nutritional Information (per 100 grams): **Calories:** 330 kcal • **Protein:** 1g • **Carbohydrates:** 2g • **Fats:** 35g • **Fiber:** 1g

17. Balsamic Vinaigrette

INGREDIENTS:

- Balsamic vinegar: 1/4 cup (60 ml)
- Olive oil: 3/4 cup (180 ml)
- Dijon mustard: 1 tsp (5 grams)
- Erythritol (or other keto sweetener): 1 tsp (4 grams)
- Garlic powder: 1/2 tsp (1 gram)
- Salt: 1/2 tsp (2 grams)
- Black pepper: 1/4 tsp (1 gram)

Cooking Tips:
• For a milder flavor, reduce the balsamic vinegar. Shake well before each use as the oil and vinegar may separate.

INSTRUCTIONS:

1. Whisk together balsamic vinegar, Dijon mustard, erythritol, garlic powder, salt, and black pepper in a bowl.
2. Slowly drizzle in olive oil while continuing to whisk until the vinaigrette is emulsified.
3. Store in an airtight container in the refrigerator.

Nutritional Information (per 100 grams): **Calories:** 700 kcal • **Protein:** 0,5g • **Carbohydrates:** 2g • **Fats:** 77g • **Fiber:** 0g

18. Cheese Sauce

INGREDIENTS:

- Heavy cream: 1 cup (240 ml)
- Cheddar cheese, shredded: 1 cup (120 grams)
- Cream cheese: 2 oz (56 grams)
- Garlic powder: 1/2 tsp (1 gram)
- Salt: 1/2 tsp (2 grams)
- Black pepper: 1/4 tsp (1 gram)

Cooking Tips:
• For a smoother sauce, ensure the cheese is fully melted and avoid overheating to prevent curdling.

INSTRUCTIONS:

1. In a saucepan, heat heavy cream over medium heat until simmering.
2. Reduce heat to low and whisk in cream cheese until smooth.
3. Gradually add shredded cheddar cheese, stirring until melted and smooth.
4. Stir in garlic powder, salt, and black pepper.
5. Continue to cook for 1-2 minutes, stirring frequently.

Nutritional Information (per 100 grams): **Calories:** 420 kcal • **Protein:** 10g • **Carbohydrates:** 4g • **Fats:** 36g • **Fiber:** 0g

Conclusion: Embrace the Keto Journey

As you close this cookbook and step into your kitchen, remember that the ketogenic diet is more than just a collection of recipes—it's a gateway to a healthier, more vibrant life. The journey you've embarked on is one of empowerment, where each meal becomes an opportunity to fuel your body with the nutrients it craves while keeping your taste buds delighted.

Transitioning to a keto lifestyle may come with its challenges, but remember that every small step forward is a victory. Start with what excites you—mastering a new recipe, experimenting with fresh ingredients, or simply savoring the energy and mental clarity that comes from nourishing your body in a whole new way.

The benefits of the keto diet go beyond weight loss; they extend to long-term health, mental sharpness, and a deeper understanding of what your body truly needs to thrive. By embracing this way of eating as a lifestyle rather than a short-term fix, you are investing in your well-being and building habits that will sustain you for years to come.

So, keep this cookbook close, revisit your favorite recipes, and don't be afraid to explore new ones. As you continue on this path, you'll discover that the ketogenic diet is not a restriction but a liberation—a way to live fully, fueled by wholesome, delicious food that supports your goals.

Here's to your continued success on this journey. May your kitchen be filled with joy, creativity, and the vibrant flavors that make keto living not just a diet, but a celebration of health and life.

Printed in Great Britain
by Amazon

48342124R00051